SpringerBriefs in Environment, Security, Development and Peace

Peace and Security Studies

Volume 11

Series editor

Hans Günter Brauch

For further volumes:
http://www.springer.com/series/13034
http://www.afes-press-books.de/html/SpringerBriefs_ESDP_MiS.htm

Sara Hellmüller · Martina Santschi
Editors

Is Local Beautiful?

Peacebuilding between International Interventions and Locally Led Initiatives

Springer

swisspeace
Schweizerische Friedensstiftung
Fondation suisse pour la paix
Fondazione svizzera per la pace
Swiss Peace Foundation

Editors
Sara Hellmüller
Martina Santschi
swisspeace
Bern
Switzerland

The cover photo was taken at Dinka Malwal, Misseriya peace conference in 2008, South Sudan, where a Misseriya and Dinka participant dance together. The photograph was taken by Martina Santschi/swisspeace who granted permission to use this photo.

ISSN 2193-3162 ISSN 2193-3170 (electronic)
ISBN 978-3-319-00305-4 ISBN 978-3-319-00306-1 (eBook)
DOI 10.1007/978-3-319-00306-1
Springer Cham Heidelberg New York Dordrecht London

Library of Congress Control Number: 2013954771

Printed on acid-free paper

Springer is part of Springer Science+Business Media (www.springer.com)

Foreword

Kwame Nkrumah, former president of Ghana, recognized the need for some type of African regional security arrangement as early as the 1960s. Ever since, slogans like 'African solutions for African problems' hit, breaking waves alike, the shores of the development assistance and peacebuilding fields. Their message was simple and crystal clear: local people know best what their problems are and therefore also know best what the appropriate solutions would be. During the past decades, the concept of local ownership—or sometimes even local leadership—which hides behind 'African solutions for African problems' has become a political mantra, both in development assistance and in peacebuilding. Since it seems to reflect nothing but common sense, one cannot even question this notion without the risk of being accused of pursuing neo-colonialist ambitions and of displaying a good deal of Western arrogance. Hence, the question *Is Local Beautiful?*, the title of the 2012 swisspeace annual conference, may sound strange to the ears of many practitioners in the field and, asked with a twinkle in the eye, even sound sacrilegious.

Local ownership was the somehow unavoidable answer to the formerly standard practice that development and peacebuilding initiatives originated in western capitals and were conceived by western experts who all too often had little knowledge of the specificities of the societies and states in which they targeted their programmes. For years now, fierce debates have been raging between the 'proponents of liberal peace' and the 'communitarians'. The former are convinced that existing universal norms orbiting around certain political and economic principles of good governance are the gold standard of peacebuilding and should be followed at all times and in all places. The latter, instead, insist that rather than relying on a universal template, sustained solutions to the problems of political order and good governance must originate within the societies themselves and take into account country-specific traditions.

The battle between those two schools of thought has not resulted in a one-sided victory—and most probably never will. While there is ample evidence that the days of traditional peacebuilding with its tool-box and one-size-fits-all approaches are numbered, experts increasingly agree that viable peacebuilding solutions need to be more pragmatic. Instead of taking either a local or an international stance in assessing peacebuilding priorities and activities, a middle ground is needed with greater focus on plurality and a careful assessment of each actor's comparative advantages (see Hellmüller, this volume).

This book grew out of the proceedings of the swisspeace annual conference 2012. Its conceptual contributions discuss the wide plethora of challenges of local ownership and suggest alternative concepts, such as political ownership, inclusiveness, honesty and partnerships. The case studies, in turn, illustrate the many successes of peace initiatives which were at various degrees locally led or locally driven. At the same time, however, they also allude to the problems which arise when it comes to putting the widely accepted local ownership paradigm into practice. Among the difficulties which we encounter over and over again, I would like to highlight just two:

First, societies in conflict affected or conflict prone regions are by no way homogeneous entities. In reality they are deeply divided into different interest groups and speak with different voices. But whose voices should be heard and prioritized among the cacophony of local owners? Don't we tend to favor the voices of groups and individuals to whom we find easy access because they share our political beliefs and cultural norms and, most of all, speak our languages?

Second, the concept of local ownership tends to assume not only that there is a minimum of social cohesion and commonality of purpose amongst local actors, but also that local owners possess the capacity and the will to pool their efforts towards the creation of a just and stable political order. In reality, though, we regularly have to realize that those capacities and capabilities, as well as the political will to build lasting peace, are rather limited.

Ever since swisspeace helped to build up the Afghan Civil Society Forum in Kabul between 2001 and 2005, we have been aware of the manifold difficulties which are entwined with the concept of local ownership. We knew from the beginning of this work that trying to impose a western-style political system upon Afghanistan was inevitably doomed to failure and therefore we decided to examine alternative ways to bring peace and stability to the country. In an attempt to strike the difficult balance between external intervention and strengthening local capacities, we helped to create the Tribal Liaison Office, thus offering a seat to the tribal elders at the negotiating table and providing an opportunity to tap into their unique knowledge and make use of their political sensitivity.

Based on this particular experience and similar endeavors in Africa, we are convinced that, in order to be successful, peacebuilding requires that all available resources are mobilized—local and international, governmental and civil society actors, business and non-profit enterprises alike. An entrepreneurial combination of external intervention and local efforts is needed, with concerted attention from the outset to finding, growing, and nurturing local capacities.

What counts in the end is to do the right things at the right time and to empower capacities for peace, wherever they are found. At the same time, it is necessary to dismantle structures that hinder progress toward building a functioning state which abides by the rule of law and puts in place the mechanisms needed to cope with conflict in a constructive, nonviolent manner. The chapters in this book confirm the validity of our arguments. At the same time they also remind us to be modest and humble about what can and cannot be achieved within the inevitably complex, politically volatile, and dynamic contexts of any peacebuilding effort.

Bern, swisspeace, July 2013 Dr. Heinz Krummenacher

Acknowledgments

The editors would like to thank the *Swiss Academy of Humanities and Social Sciences* (SAGW) and the Support Association of swisspeace for providing generous funding for the swisspeace annual conference, Dr. Briony Jones for proof-reading the articles and Dr. Hans Günter Brauch, the ESDP series editor, and the Springer teams in Heidelberg (Germany) and Chennai (India) for publishing this volume.

swisspeace annual conference 2012, Bern. *Source* swisspeace. Permission to use this photo was granted.

swisspeace annual conference 2012, Bern. *Source* swisspeace. Permission to use this photo was granted.

swisspeace annual conference 2012, Bern. *Source* swisspeace. Permission to use this photo was granted.

swisspeace annual conference 2012, Bern. *Source* swisspeace. Permission to use this photo was granted.

swisspeace annual conference 2012, Bern. *Source* swisspeace. Permission to use this photo was granted.

Contents

Introduction

Sara Hellmüller

The title of the 2012 swisspeace annual conference and this subsequent publication point to the challenges in balancing external interventions and locally led initiatives. International peacebuilding has become prominent since the term was famously defined by former UN Secretary General Boutros-Boutros Ghali in his Agenda for Peace as "[a]ction to identify and support structures which will tend to strengthen and solidify peace" (Boutros-Boutros 1992: §21). Initially considered as applying only to post-conflict transitions, the Supplement to an Agenda for Peace (1995) extended the term "across the conflict spectrum of pre-conflict prevention, actions during warfare, and post-conflict measures" (Call and Cousens 2007: 2). Peacebuilding involves a wide range of activities such as security, establishing socioeconomic foundations, a political framework, fostering reconciliation, healing of the wounds of war and justice initiatives (see e.g., Smith 2004: 27; Chetail 2009: 8; Barnett et al. 2007: 49f). Since the mid-1990s, international peacebuilding has become increasingly professionalised as these different activities have been integrated into the policies and programs of international organizations, bilateral donors, and NGOs (Goetschel and Hagman 2009: 56).

The international peacebuilding field has developed concomitantly with a strong belief in liberal peace theory since the end of the Cold War (Donais 2012: 22). The dominant conviction assumes that political and economic liberalization form the exclusive recipe to prevent and address conflicts and solve problems of under-development (Paris 2011: 32). The intellectual roots of liberal peace theory go back further, however, with their origins in the philosophy of Kant and his assertion that free trade between states in conjunction with a democratic government will lead to peace (Gilady and Russett 2002: 393; Paris 2004: 41). Later theorists took up Kant's ideas and asserted that democracies indeed do not go to war against each other (Doyle 1983; Russett 1993; Ray 1995). Their explanation is threefold. First, due to the fact that in democracies it is the people who decide whether or not to go to war, they will decide against war because they are the ones who will suffer most from it. Second, states that are economically and commercially interdependent will not fight each other because it runs counter to their interests. And finally, democratic states' fundamental values of compromise and plurality are also carried into their international relations (Bellamy et al. 2004: 26; Hameiri 2011: 191; Doyle 1983; Russett 1993; Ray 1995; Newman et al. 2009:

11). These arguments have led to the belief that societies which are organized according to liberal principles tend to be more peaceful than illiberal states, both in their domestic realms and in their international relations (Newman et al. 2009: 11). Peacebuilding has thus become liberal in character (Paris 2004; Richmond 2004; Barnett 2006; Zaum 2012). Thereby, its activities have increasingly gone beyond the pacification and stabilization of a conflict context, and have come to involve the instalment of a well functioning democracy and market economy.Such increased interventionism to promote these goals is also at the core of the many critiques that have been directed toward liberal peacebuilding. The establishment of transitional administrations in East Timor and Kosovo where the international community exercised governmental power have in particular prompted substantial debates on the extent of international authority (Zaum 2006: 455; Bellamy 2010: 194; von Billerbeck 2011: 332; Chesterman 2007: 5). An attempt to make liberal peacebuilding more legitimate and to balance its interventionist tendencies can be seen in a stronger emphasis now placed on integrating affected communities (Miall et al. 1999: 18). Thereby, local ownership has become a frequently used term in peacebuilding debates with "an established moral power" (Shinoda 2008: 4). It refers to "the capacities of political, social, and community actors in a particular country [...] to set, and take responsibility for, the peacebuilding agenda and to muster and sustain support for it" (Pouligny 2009: 174). The origins of the term lie in the field of development cooperation (Saxby 2003; von Billerbeck 2011). The Development Assistance Committee of the Organization for Economic Cooperation and Development stated in 1996 that sustainable development "must be locally owned" (OECD DAC 1996: 17). Similarly, James Wolfensohn (1999), former director of the World Bank, stated that "countries must be in the driver's seat and set the course" by determining the "goals and the phasing, timing and sequencing of programmes". The sustainability of development programmes thus came to be seen as contingent upon the way in which they were owned by local actors. This approach was taken up in the international peacebuilding field in the late 1990s. Former UN Secretary General Kofi Annan (2001) stated that domestic peace "can only be achieved by the local population itself; the role of the United Nations is merely to facilitate the process that seeks to dismantle the structures of violence and create the conditions conducive to durable peace and sustainable development".

Despite the rhetorical adherence to local ownership, however, most international organizations involved in peacebuilding still take on a top-down approach in their intervention and explicitly or implicitly impose western concepts upon societies (Autesserre 2010; Zaum 2012; Goetschel and Hagman 2009). Often times, international actors, along with national elites that have been co-opted into western schemes, decide where to set the priorities and devise corresponding strategies (Mac Ginty 2008: 142). Several authors have criticized the civilizing nature of liberal peacebuilding, also termed "conflict management imperialism" (Rupesinghe 1995: 316). They point to the fact that international peacebuilders have usually underestimated the importance of local acceptance and imposed a template approach ignoring the specificities of the respective conflict context while imposing western liberal concepts upon the local population. Such an imposition also involves the risk that international peacebuilding efforts are not in line with or even counteract local peace initiatives.

Indeed, such initiatives are often overlooked. As Pearce (1997: 451) states, external peacebuilding agencies tend to "focus the debate on their interventions … and much less on the dynamic of local capacities and how they can shape the future prospects for peace-building". This is illustrated by the fact that peacebuilding is often inherently defined as being conducted by *international*, rather than by *local* actors and agency ascribed almost exclusively to the international level (cf. Donais 2012: 28; Barnett et al. 2007: 36; Call and Cook 2003: 238). Therefore, "little serious thought has been devoted to the question of what configuration of locally owned and externally driven is most likely to shift societies decisively from war to peace" (Donais 2012: 2). This is surprising given the frequent reference to local ownership and the wide acceptance of the positive link between a well managed cooperation between international and local actors and an increased effectiveness of peacebuilding (Anderson and Olson 2003: 37). As Goodhand and Walton (2009: 308) state, there is a need "to better disaggregate the domestic and international arenas and the complex interface between them".

This book seeks to address this need by providing insights into the complex interactions between international and local actors from multiple perspectives. In doing so, it discusses which types of relations between them are supportive for the fostering of sustainable peace. It addresses the conceptual and theoretical challenges associated with the concept of local ownership and asks the question of what 'local' means in the peacebuilding and development context, which actors on the ground actually represent the local level and how external actors choose their partners from amongst them. Moreover, it assesses the potential of locally led initiatives and local conflict resolution mechanisms and their interaction with external interventions. Several authors provide insights into these questions and introduce more nuances into our thinking about both locally led initiatives and external interventions. As such, this book aims to encourage critical reflections on these topical debates in peacebuilding and development.

The book is divided into two parts. First, conceptual contributions raise critical questions about the concept of local ownership and propose alternatives. Second, case studies of DR Congo, South Sudan, Switzerland, and Myanmar examine how local conflict resolution mechanisms contribute to peacebuilding and how the interaction between local and international actors plays out in practice.

References

Anderson, Mary B.; Olson, Lara, 2003: "Confronting War: Critical Lessons for Peace Practitioners", in: *Reflecting on Peace Practice Project* (Cambridge: The Collaborative for Development Action, Inc.).

Annan, Kofi, 2001: "Report of the Secretary General, No exit without strategy: Security Council decision-making and the closure or transition of United Nations peacekeeping operations", *UN Doc.* S/2001/394 (New York: United Nations).

Autesserre, Séverine, 2010: *The Trouble with the Congo: Local Violence and the Failure of International Peacebuilding* (New York: Cambridge University Press).

Barnett, Michael, 2006: "Building a Republican Peace: Stabilizing States after War", in: *International Security*, 30, 4: 87–112.

Barnett, Michael; Kim, Hunjoon; O'Donnell, Madalene; Sitea, Laura, 2007: "Peacebuilding: What Is in a Name?", in: *Global Governance*, 13: 35–58.

Bellamy, Alex J., 2010: "The Institutionalisation of peacebuilding: what role for the UN Peacebuilding Commission?", in: Richmond, Oliver (Ed.): *Palgrave Advances in Peacebuilding: Critical Developments and Approaches* (Basingstoke; New York: Palgrave Macmillan): 193–212.

Bellamy, Alex J.; Williams, Paul; Griffin, Stuart, 2004: *Understanding Peacekeeping* (Cambridge: Polity Press).

Boutros-Boutros, Ghali, 1992, "An Agenda for Peace: Preventive diplomacy, peacemaking and peace-keeping", *Report of the Secretary-General pursuant to the statement adopted by the Summit Meeting of the Security Council on 31 January 1992.*

Call, Charles T.; Cook, Susan E., 2003: "On Democratization and Peacebuilding", in: *Global Governance*, 9, 2: 233–246.

Call, Charles T.; Cousens, Elizabeth M., 2007: "Ending Wars and Building Peace", in: *Coping with Crisis - Working Paper Series* (New York: International Peace Academy).

Chesterman, Simon, 2007: "Ownership in Theory and in Practice: Transfer of Authority in UN Statebuilding Operations", in: *Journal of Intervention and Statebuilding*, 1, 1: 3–26.

Chetail, Vincent, 2009: "Introduction: Post-Conflict Peacebuilding - Ambiguity and Identity", in: Chetail, Vincent (Ed.): *Post-Conflict Peacebuilding. A Lexicon* (Oxford: Oxford University Press): 1–33.

Donais, Timothy, 2012: *Peacebuilding and Local Ownership - Post-conflict consensus building* (London and New York: Routledge Taylor & Francis Group).

Doyle, Michael W., 1983: "Kant, Liberal Legacies, and Foreign Affairs", in: *Philosophy & Public Affairs*, 12, 3: 205–235.

Francis, Diana, 2002, *People, Peace and Power: Conflict Transformation in Action* (London: Pluto Press).

Gilady, Lilach; Russett, Bruce, 2002: "Peacemaking and Conflict Resolution", in: Carlsnaes, Walter; Risse, Thomas; Simmons, Beth A. (Eds.): *Handbook of International Relations* (London: Sage Publications): 392–408.

Goetschel, Laurent; Hagman, Tobias, 2009: "Civilian Peacebuilding: peace by bureaucratic means?", in: *Conflict, Security & Development*, 9, 1: 55–73.

Goodhand, Jonathan; Walton, Oliver, 2009: "The Limits of Liberal Peacebuilding? International Engagement in the Sri Lankan Peace Process", in: *Journal of Intervention and Statebuilding*, 3, 3: 303–323.

Haider, Huma, 2009: "Community-based Approaches to Peacebuilding in Conflict-affected and Fragile Contexts", in: *Issues Paper* (Birmingham: Governance and Social Development Resource Center).

Hameiri, Shahar, 2011: "A Reality Check for the Critique of the Liberal Peace", in: Campbell, Susanna; Chandler, David; Sabaratnam, Meera (Eds.): *A Liberal Peace?: The Problems and Practices of Peacebuilding* (London: Zed Books): 191–208.

Hansen, Annika S., 2008: "Local Ownership in Peace Operations", in: Donais, Timothy (Ed.): *Local Ownership and Security Sector Reform* (Berlin: Lit Verlag).

Mac Ginty, Roger, 2008: "Indigenous Peace-Making Versus the Liberal Peace", in: *Cooperation and Conflict: Journal of the Nordic International Studies Association*, 43, 2: 139–163.

McCandless, Erin; Abu-Nimer, Mohammed, 2006: "National Ownership in Security, Peacebuilding and Development: Grassroots Activism, Institution Building and Policy Making", in: *Journal of Peacebuilding & Development*, 2, 3: 1–6.

Miall, Hugh; Ramsbotham, Oliver; Woodhouse, Tom, 1999: *Contemporary Conflict Resolution. The prevention, management and transformation of deadly conflicts* (Cambridge: Polity Press).

Newman, Edward; Paris, Roland; Richmond, Oliver, 2009: *New perspectives on liberal peacebuilding* (New York: United Nations University Press).

Odendaal, Andries; Olivier, Retief, 2008: "Local Peace Committees: Some Reflections and Lessons Learnt", in: *Study Report* (Kathmandu: AED, USAID).

OECD DAC, 1996: *Shaping the 21st Century: The Contribution of Development Co-operation* (Paris: Organisation for Economic Cooperation and Development).

Paris, Roland, 2004: *At War's End: Building Peace after Civil Conflict* (Cambridge: Cambridge University Press).

Paris, Roland, 2010: "Saving Liberal Peacebuilding", in: *The Review of International Studies*, 36, 2: 337–365.

Paris, Roland, 2011, "Critiques of Liberal Peace", in: Campbell, Susanna; Chandler, David; Sabaratnam, Meera (Eds.): *A Liberal Peace?: The Problems and Practices of Peacebuilding* (London: Zed Books): 31–51.

Pearce, Jenny, 1997: "Sustainable Peace-Building in the South: Experiences from Latin America", in: *Development in Practice*, 7, 4: 438–455.

Pouligny, Béatrice, 2009: "Local Ownership", in: Chetail, Vincent (Ed.): *Post-Conflict Peacebuilding. A Lexicon* (Oxford: Oxford University Press): 174–187.

Prendergast, John; Plumb, Emily, 2002: "Building Local Capacity: From Implementation to Peacebuilding", in: Stedman, S.J. (Ed.): *Ending Civil Wars* (Boulder. Co: Rienner).

Ray, James Lee, 1995: *Democracy and International Conflict* (Columbia: University of South Carolina Press).

Richmond, Oliver, 2004: "The Globalization of Responses to Conflict and the Peacebuilding Consensus", in: *Cooperation and Conflict: Journal of the Nordic International Studies Association*, 39, 2: 129–150.

Richmond, Oliver, 2010: "What is your alternative?"; in: *openDemocracy*; at:< http://www.opendemocracy.net/oliver-p-richmond/what-is-your-alternative>.

Rupesinghe, Kumar, 1995: "Transformation innerstaatlicher Konflikte: Von 'Problemlösungs-Workshops' zu Friedensallianzen", in: Ropers, Norbert; Debiel, Tobias (Eds.): *Friedliche Konfliktbearbeitung in der Staaten- und Gesellschaftswelt* (Bonn: Stiftung Entwicklung und Frieden): 304–321.

Russett, Bruce, 1993: *Grasping the Democratic Peace: Principles for a Post-Cold War World* (Princeton: Princeton University Press).

Saxby, John, 2003: *Local ownership and development co-operation - the role of Northern civil society* (Ontario: Canadian Council for International Co-operation Resource Document).

Shinoda, Hideaki, 2008: "The Difficulty and Importance of Local Ownership and Capacity Development in Peacebuilding", in: *Hiroshima Peace Science*, 30: 95–115.

Smith, Dan, 2004: *Towards a Strategic Framework for Peacebuilding: Getting Their Act Together* (Oslo: PRIO - International Peace Research Institute).

Tongeren, Paul van., 2005: *People building peace II : successful stories of civil society* (Boulder: Lynne Rienner).

Billerbeck, Sarah B.K. von, 2011: "Whose Peace? Local Ownership and UN Peacebuilding", in: *Journal of Intervention and Statebuilding*, Special Issue: 322–365.

Wolfensohn, James D., 1999: *A Proposal for a Comprehensive Development Framework* (Washington DC: The World Bank).
Zaum, Dominik, 2006: "The authority of international administrations in international society", in: *Review of International Studies*, 32, 3: 455–73.
Zaum, Dominik, 2012: "Beyond the 'Liberal Peace'" in: *Global Governance*, 18, 1: 121–32.

swisspeace annual conference 2012, Bern. *Source* swisspeace. Permission to use this photo was granted.

Part I
Conceptual Contributions

Participants at a negotiation training in Yangon, Myanmar. *Source* Rachel Gasser/swisspeace. The permission to reproduce this photograph was granted.

Chapter 1
Owners or Partners? A Critical Analysis of the Concept of Local Ownership

Sara Hellmüller

Abstract This chapter critically examines the term local ownership. It shows that while the concept is widely used and accepted in policy debates, many international peacebuilding programmes are still largely externally designed in practice. Due to the dominance of the liberal peace paradigm in contemporary peacebuilding debates, this means that such programmes are heavily influenced by liberal principles. At the same time, local initiatives are assessed based on their compatibility with liberal values. An alternative is provided by communitarian approaches which suggest taking the local as a starting point. In this view, the role of international actors is merely to support strategies already undertaken by local actors. Based on empirical insights, this chapter questions however whether in this latter case, local ownership is still relevant as a concept or whether it would not be more accurate to talk about local leadership. It then proposes a middle ground between liberal and communitarian approaches by examining the interaction between external and internal actors. Thereby, it suggests partnerships based on a greater focus on plurality and each actor's comparative advantages. Only in such a way, the chapter concludes, does peacebuilding revolve around a true cooperation between international and local actors while respecting each actor's unique perspectives.

Keywords Local ownership · Local peacebuilding · Liberal peace theory · Communitarian approaches · Cooperation between local and international actors

S. Hellmüller (✉)
swisspeace, Bern, Switzerland
University of Basel, Basel, Switzerland
e-mail: sara.hellmueller@swisspeace.ch

S. Hellmüller and M. Santschi (eds.), *Is Local Beautiful?*,
SpringerBriefs in Environment, Security, Development and Peace 11,
DOI: 10.1007/978-3-319-00306-1_1, © The Author(s) 2014

1.1 Introduction

The balance between external interventions and locally led peace initiatives is not easily struck. From an international perspective, the UN Charter proclaims the sacrosanct principle of sovereign equality and non-intervention into the domestic affairs of member states on the one hand. On the other hand, however, the UN Security Council has the competence to identify threats to international peace and security and take the appropriate measures to maintain or restore order (Charter of the United Nations 1945) and thus holds the international "monopoly of the legitimate use of force" (Chetail 2004: 81). References to the concept of local ownership have been used to nuance this dilemma. The nurturing of local acceptance to external interventions seeks to—at least rhetorically—attenuate their intrusiveness. As Von Billerbeck (2011: 326) notes, "the UN's dedication to local ownership represents an attempt to reconcile incompatible institutional norms relating to sovereignty and international security through an expansion of the principle of consent to peace operations". However, local ownership has been insufficiently defined and rarely thoroughly implemented in practice. Moreover, it remains ambiguous as to whether it actually attenuates the balancing act between external intervention and locally led initiatives or whether it is a concept which is already inherently biased towards external actors.

This chapter critically reflects on these aspects. In its first part, it assesses the term of local ownership and argues that in its current embedding within the liberal peace paradigm it is inherently biased towards external perspectives. Communitarian approaches provide an alternative to the liberal reading of local ownership by taking local norms and traditions as the starting point. The present chapter proposes a middle ground consisting of a more nuanced analysis of the interaction between external and internal actors which takes neither as starting point, but is seen as shaped by a multitude of perspectives. Such an approach is presented in more detail in the second part of the chapter. It recommends assessing the interaction between external and internal actors according to the specific context and focusing on the respective comparative advantages that each actor has.

1.2 From Local Ownership...

1.2.1 Critiques of Local Ownership

The frequent reference to local ownership in current peacebuilding debates is based on the agreement between different scholars and practitioners that in the endeavour to build lasting peace, the involvement of the affected communities is indispensable (Reich 2006: 1; Suhrke 2007; Sending 2009). The underlying, and rather intuitive, assumption is that a process not owned by the people who are affected by it will not be sustainable in the long term (Newman et al. 2009: 4).

Despite its wide acceptance, however, the concept of local ownership has also attracted criticism. While the intrinsic value of local ownership is rarely disputed, its practical use and implications have been questioned (Pouligny 2009: 175).

Three main strands of critiques can be identified. First, authors point to the risk that the international community uses the concept in order to withdraw from a context too early by referring to the need for more local ownership (Reich 2006; Jarstad/Olsson 2011). Second, local ownership can allegedly be instrumentalized to obscure the intrusiveness of an international intervention and to justify its continued presence by asserting that local ownership will be established as soon as conditions permit (Kuehne et al. 2008). Third, and arguably most importantly, local ownership is often seen as a buzzword used to satisfy donor demands with empty words (Scheye/Peake 2005: 232; Chesterman 2007: 8; Zimmermann 2007: 3), but which has rarely been substantively implemented in practice (Pietz/von Carlowitz 2007: 6; Saxby 2003; Von Billerbeck 2011: 330). Indeed, the international tendency remains to design peacebuilding projects without significant local inputs. As Donais (2012: 1) states, recent peacebuilding operations "have tended to more closely resemble externally driven exercises in statebuilding and social engineering than patient, elicitive processes of peace nurturing". The continued presence of armed groups, framing of the conflict states as failed and pathologization of conflict societies are used as arguments for more international assertiveness in peacebuilding interventions (Hansen 2008: 41; Woodward 2006; Hughes/Pupavac 2005; Marenin 2005: 18). To be sure, promoting local ownership, especially when fighting is still ongoing, is a challenging task. In the initial stages of a peace process for instance, the international community usually mainly interacts with armed elite actors (Ramsbotham et al. 2005: 201). Mobilizing civil society and collecting the views of the citizens demands time and is often considered an almost insurmountable practical task at this stage. Hence, decisions tend to be taken during negotiations which may not correspond to the immediate priorities of the population. As Rogier (2004: 39) has argued "even if an 'elite pact' might be necessary to end the war, it is not sufficient to build peace". Such an approach and absence of meaningfully implementing the concept of local ownership into practice has resulted in peacebuilding operations reflecting the current state of the art in peacebuilding debates rather than realities on the ground (Lidén 2005: 10; Bellamy 2004: 28). This state of the art has been heavily influenced by the liberal peace paradigm.

According to the liberal peace paradigm, examining local ownership signifies looking at how international programmes are received, interpreted and sustained by local actors (Reich 2006; Hansen 2008; Donais2009a, b). This vision takes international programmes as starting points and then seeks to inquire whether and how they become locally owned. In that sense, it means "'their' ownership of 'our' ideas" (Suhrke 2007: 1292). Based on such critiques, the liberal peace paradigm has been accused of promoting a vision of local ownership which supposes that local actors will take ownership over a pre-defined (liberal) vision of peacebuilding (Donais 2009a: 6). As de Heredia (2009: 2) notes, local ownership "has re-stated the leading role of international actors above local actors" and "has implied that local actors should eventually own a process that the international community has drafted for them". Thus, in its current use and embedding within the liberal peace paradigm, local ownership can arguably be said to be a concept which is biased towards an international perspective given that the international community enjoys most of the decision-making power in the design of programmes that local communities should own in the end. Therefore it has become a largely externally-driven concept which loses its importance outside of an authoritative international intervention due to the fact that 'ownership' is defined largely as 'buy-in' (Donais 2012: 71).

1.2.2 A Viable Alternative?

The communitarian approach presents an alternative vision of local ownership by taking the local level as the starting point (Donais 2012: 5). In this view, the situation in the host countries is taken as the "'natural' state of affairs" (Lidén 2005: 45). In contrast to the liberal peace which pretends to promote universal templates (Sending 2009: 7), the communitarian approach claims that external interventions should be based on the traditions and cultures in the host countries and initiatives already undertaken should be adequately supported (Lidén 2005: 47). One could ask, however, if adopting a communitarian approach and seeing local conditions as the starting point upon which international peacekeeping actors should build, what relevance does the concept of local ownership retain? If local actors are in the driving seat and decide upon the design and implementation of programmes, would these programmes not by their very design be locally owned? And would it, in this case, not be more consistent to talk about local leadership?

These rhetorical questions suggest that discussions about local ownership are relevant only in cases in which international, rather than local actors, decide over the design of a peacebuilding process. Where the local context is taken as the starting point and initiatives already undertaken locally are merely supported by international actors, the ownership question as defined in the liberal peace paradigm loses much of its pertinence. Therefore, this chapter suggests that rather than focusing on how to promote local buy-in to international concepts and programmes, what is needed is a rethink of what is taken as the starting point. Thereby, it takes the middle ground between communitarian and liberal conceptualizations of local ownership by putting a focus on the interaction between external and internal actors from a multitude of perspectives, rather than mainly from an international or a local standpoint. It calls for what Donais (2012: 145) has termed "an attitudinal shift on the part of international actors toward fully embracing the notion of peacebuilding as a genuine partnership across the international-local divide". In that sense, neither the local nor the international level is taken as the starting point, but peacebuilding priorities and activities are formed and constantly reshaped through their interaction. This interaction needs to be defined according to the specific context in which the intervention takes place and be based on each actor's comparative advantages. These two aspects are examined in what follows.

1.3 …to Partnerships?

1.3.1 Context-specific Assessment of Partnerships

An assessment of the interaction between different actors in their specific peacebuilding context starts with the acknowledgement of plurality. Both categories, the external and internal, are made up of a multitude of actors with different perceptions, experiences, interests and positions and neither "represents a homogeneous or unified set of actors" (Donais 2012: 37). For instance, the meaning that 'peace' has for a specific group is influenced by their respective perspectives on a conflict. These perspectives are formed in dynamic processes and depend on social, cultural, as well as historical factors. Therefore, it is crucially important to look at power and socio-cultural dynamics in a country (Sending 2010: 38) and to carefully examine whose views are taken as representative. National elites' approaches, for instance, are sometimes more closely aligned with western views than with the ones of their co-citizens. Thus, the dichotomy between international and local actors that is often intuitively assumed should be broken up.

Assessing partnerships between external and internal actors in their specific context also helps to take into account and built upon peacebuilding initiatives already undertaken locally. Several authors have studied such local initiatives (Prendergast/Plumb 2002; Francis 2002; Tongeren 2005; McCandless/Abu-Nimer 2006; Haider 2009) and comparative analyses have shown that they can make a difference for peace in a post-conflict society (Tongeren 1999, 2005: 1; Kang et al. 2009). These local resources often remain underutilized, however, as peacebuilding is mostly defined as being conducted by external actors. As Donais (2012: 30) puts it, "'the local' generally appears as the object of peacebuilding rather than as the subject". However, rather than superseded, local resources should be supported and valorised (Pouligny 2005: 503). A peacebuilding programme should be the result of constant negotiations and interactions between local and international values rather than the domination of one over the other.

At the same time, it is important to not naively glorify local approaches (Mac Ginty 2008: 149; Betts 2005: 748; Carl 2003: 3). Rather, we should assess these capacities in their historical, social and political setting. Different groups may start to refer to traditional institutions and practices as they want to benefit from the "supposed higher moral value to be gained by labelling a practice or attitude as 'traditional'" (Mac Ginty 2008: 150). Often, certain actors even start to mirror western society in the hope of benefitting from the association with western donors. In that sense, the realm of peacebuilding is used as an arena of political positioning. As Smith (2004: 27) states "[t]he lines of division that led to conflict escalation normally survive the peace process: if war is continuation of politics by other means, peace is generally the resumption of the same politics, often by the same pre-war means".

It is clear that the proposed shift to a negotiating, rather than imposing, attitude also implies compromises as in some cases local and international values might be outright incompatible. As Donais (2012: 152) states "[w]hile the acceptance of existing political realities almost necessarily entails painful compromises with key international norms, it may be balanced over time by successful efforts to set in motion dynamics through which change can gradually emerge from within". Therefore, a substantial amount of time and patience is needed in order to understand local political configurations and to identify valuable partners. This is not an easy task and also depends on the issue area (Paris/Sisk 2007: 6). In general, the most immediate partner, especially for intergovernmental actors such as the UN is usually the national government (Autesserre 2010: 94–96; Von Billerbeck 2011: 339). This is due to the principle of state sovereignty and the risk of delegitimizing the government by circumventing it to engage directly with local actors (Brinkerhoff 2007: 117). However, it is important to go beyond these national elites which means engaging with actors at the more local level. Besides the population in general, such actors include local organizations who are already undertaking peacebuilding projects. This is what the next section turns to.

1.3.2 A Place for Everyone

This section analyses the interaction between international and local peacebuilding actors. Local peacebuilding organizations are not to be confused with civil society more generally although they are part of the latter. The focus here is on those local actors who implement projects aimed at promoting peace, sometimes in the form of several individuals working together in a loose association, sometimes more institutionalized and nationally recognized. Such local capacities are often overlooked in theory and practice. For instance, studies on how different *international* actors, i.e. UN agencies, UN peacekeeping missions and international NGOs, coordinate their activities amongst each other (e.g. Natsios 1995; Cooley/Ron 2002; Ricigliano 2003) are much more frequent than how each one of them interacts with local peacebuilding actors. In practice, coordination between international actors in peacebuilding has often become hugely "introspective and focused on its inner workings" at the risk of excluding local actors (Hansen 2008: 53). This often leads to the creation of an international bubble in a localized context and an ignorance of how local and international peacebuilding actors could better work together. The power balance might well remain tilted towards the international actors as they control the flow of money (Van Brabant 2010: 8). However, local actors arguably also dispose of leverage as it has now been widely acknowledged that peacebuilding programmes cannot succeed in the long term without their support and commitment. As Anderson and Olson (2003: 37) state "when they work together insiders and outsiders bring different and distinct qualities to peace partnerships". Thus, a detailed analysis of the comparative advantages of each set of actors can help for each one to find its place and to not duplicate tasks. While such advantages and roles are clearly context-specific, the situation in Ituri (DR Congo) serves as an example of what different actors see as their own role and that of their potential partners.[1]

The perceived comparative advantages of international actors can be summarized in four points. First, international actors are often seen as valuable outsiders when impartial forces are difficult to find from within the conflict context (Joseph 2007: 109; Interview #5 2011; Interview #17 2011). An external intervention is usually considered necessary in the beginning in order to stabilize a region and to create the space for longer term approaches (Hansen 2008: 49). A second advantage mentioned is the fact that international structures often have the capacities to implement large-scale projects. They are familiar with fundraising procedures and can thus mobilize substantial amounts of money (Interview #21 2011). Third, they are perceived as bringing expertise on how to respond to conflicts (Interview #12 2011). Even though they might have gathered these experiences in other contexts, lessons can still be drawn and capacities and skills transferred–after the necessary adaptations and with the required humility. Fourth, being present due to the invitation (or at least acceptance) of the host government, international actors are also said to have privileged access to national authorities (Interview #10 2011; Interview #11 2011). Therefore, they are seen as being in a position to facilitate the relations between local NGOs and international donors on the one hand and local NGOs and national authorities on the other hand. With regard to donors, international peacebuilding actors can share their expertise in project management and fundraising and support local actors in becoming more easily eligible for funds granted by international donors (Interview #95 2012). Concerning national authorities, local NGOs often face constraints in their influence at the national level. International peacebuilding actors, due to their privileged access to state structures, can facilitate these relationships (Interview #10 2011; Interview #11 2011). This also helps to guard against the danger of reducing the accountability of the state. This phenomenon can occur in protracted conflict situations in which the international community assumes state functions. In Ituri, for instance, it is often the case that claims for infrastructure and social services, such as schools, hospitals or roads, are not directed at the government anymore, but at international actors (Interviews and Focus Group Discussions, Spring 2011:12; Interview #26 2012). Such structures should not be eternalized and the state should take up its responsibility once in a position to do so (Brinkerhoff 2007: 117). If external actors facilitate the contact and information flow between state

[1] What follows is a compilation of international and local perspectives on the issue in question assessed through in-depth interviews and focus group discussions in Ituri (2011/2012). Translations of citations from French to English were made by the author.

authorities and local NGOs, the latter can improve their channels for advocacy and increase responsibilities taken by the government which, in the long run, contributes to localizing peacebuilding (Interview #82 2012). Moreover, linking local peacebuilding actors to government structures can help render their initiatives nationally relevant. This, in turn, potentially increases their legitimacy in the eyes of international donors.

Turning to the perceived comparative advantages of local peacebuilding actors, first, their work is seen as having a big symbolic impact (besides the more tangible ones) during an armed conflict. If the population realizes that some of their compatriots have started working for peace, it usually sends a stronger message than if international actors implement similar peacebuilding activities (Focus Group Discussion #1 2011). Second, having lived through the conflict, they enjoy a lot of credibility and legitimacy. As one interviewee put it "international actors act by what they have heard, we act according to what we have seen and lived" (Focus Group Discussion #1 2011). This credibility is further enhanced by the fact that beneficiaries know that they will stay in the area even if donors withdraw. This creates trust in their approach as they themselves have to live with the consequences of their own programmes. Moreover, local peacebuilding actors speak the language and know the cultural specificities of the conflict context (Interview #8 2011). Thus, they "provide an intuitive understanding of local conditions that international NGOs could not hope to equal" (Natsios 1995: 410). Thirdly, they are usually more cost-effective (Interview #2 2011; Focus Group Discussion #3 2011). They can implement projects without large bureaucratic procedures and operate from modest offices with limited logistics. Fourth, they also have access to remote areas where the international community is not present due to security restrictions (Interview #15 2011). As such, local NGOs can act as intermediaries between the local population and international peacebuilding actors, using their language skills, education, and positioning which allow them access to both communities (Interview #4 2011; Informal Discussion #23 2011). They can assist international actors in making their programmes more locally relevant. This does not mean that local peacebuilding actors come to be equated with the local population and are seen as perfect representatives of the latter. There are more and less legitimate ones which brings us back to the heterogeneity of actors and the importance of identifying valuable partners. Rather, local peacebuilding actors can play bridging roles, by facilitating contacts and access to local communities. It is clear and pragmatic to approach people who speak the same language and who know how to navigate the space between the local and the international in the beginning. However, it is important that international actors also break free from their golden cages to experience reality on the ground. This does not mean that they should start to engage directly in local conflict resolution. They have neither the authority nor the legitimacy to address long-standing social conflicts. However, they should develop knowledge on the context and its people to act in an informed and relevant way.

The above shows that both sets of actors have specific advantages and roles they can take up. This is confirmed by the fact that when asked about the role for international and local peacebuilding actors, interviewees in Ituri clearly stated that everyone has a place to contribute to peace. As one observer said, "peace in Ituri has many fathers, everyone has contributed" (Interview #5 2011).

1.4 Conclusion

This chapter has critically analysed the term local ownership. It has shown that while there is widespread agreement on the importance of the concept in theory, the same does not hold in practice where peacebuilding programmes are still largely internationally designed. In the contemporary world, this means that peacebuilding programmes are heavily influenced by the liberal peace paradigm and local initiatives are assessed according to their compatibility with liberal values. In an alternative approach to peacebuilding, the communitarian view, the local is taken as the starting point and the role of international actors is to support what is already undertaken by local actors. The chapter questioned, based on empirical insights, whether in this case we can still talk about local ownership or whether it would not be more consistent to talk about local leadership. It then proposed a middle ground in the assessment of the interaction between external and internal peacebuilding actors based on partnerships with a call for a greater focus on plurality and a careful assessment of each actor's comparative advantages. Only like this, does peacebuilding revolve around a true cooperation between external and internal actors while respecting each actor's unique perspectives.

References

Anderson, Mary B.; Olson, Lara, 2003: *Confronting War: Critical Lessons for Peace Practitioners* (Cambridge, MA: Reflecting on Peace Practice Project, The Collaborative for Development Action, Inc).

Autesserre, Séverine, 2010: *The Trouble with the Congo: Local Violence and the Failure of International Peacebuilding* (New York: Cambridge University Press).

Bellamy, Alex J., 2004: "The 'Next Stage' in Peace Operations Theory?", in: *International Peacekeeping*, 11, 1: 17–38.

Betts, Alexander, 2005: "Should Approaches to Post-conflict Justice and Reconciliation be Determined Globally, Nationally or Locally?", in: *European Journal of Development Research*, 17, 4: 735–752.

Brinkerhoff, Derik W., 2007: "Where There's a Will, There's a Way? Untangling Ownership and Political Will in Post-Conflict Stability and Reconstruction Operations", in: *The Whitehead Journal of Diplomacy and International Relations*, 8, 1: 111–120.

Carl, Andy, 2003: "Supporting local capacities for handling violent conflict: a role for international NGOs?", in: Conciliation Resources (Ed.): *Occasional Paper* (London: Conciliation Resources).

Charter of the United Nations 1945; at: http://www.un.org/en/documents/charter/index.shtml (10 January 2013).
Chesterman, Simon, 2007: "Ownership in Theory and in Practice: Transfer of Authority in UN Statebuilding Operations", in: *Journal of Intervention and Statebuilding*, 1, 1: 3–26.
Chetail, Vincent, 2004: "Ad-Hocism and the rules of Collective Security: Is Peacekeeping still relevant for maintaining international peace and security?", in: *Refugee Survey Quarterly*, 23, 4: 77–110.
Cooley, Alexander; Ron, James, 2002: "The NGO Scramble: Organizational Insecurity and the Political Economy of Transnational Action", in: *International Security*, 27, 1: 5–39.
de Heredia, Marta Iñiguez, 2009: "The space for Congolese self-determination absences and presences of the African Union and the United Nations", in: *African Journal of Political Science and International Relations*, 3, 1: 1–14.
Donais, Timothy, 2009a: "Empowerment or Imposition? Dilemmas of Local Ownership in Post-Conflict Peacebuilding Processes", in: *Peace & Change*, 34, 1: 3–26.
Donais, Timothy, 2009b: "Inclusion or Exclusion? Local Ownership and Security Sector Reform", in: *Studies in Social Justice*, 3, 1: 117–131.
Donais, Timothy, 2012: "Peacebuilding and Local Ownership - Post-conflict consensus building", in: Krause, Keith; Biersteker, Thomas J.; Bocco, Ricardo (Eds.): *Studies in Conflict, Development and Peacebuilding* (London – New York: Routledge Taylor & Francis Group).
Focus Group Discussion #1, 2011: Local NGO Representatives 1_FGD_Bu_III_Ca. Ituri.
Focus Group Discussion #3, 2011: Professor and Civil Society Representative 3_FGD_Bu_III_BbC. Ituri.
Francis, Diana, 2002: *People, Peace and Power: Conflict Transformation in Action* (London: Pluto Press).
Haider, Huma, 2009: "Community-based Approaches to Peacebuilding in Conflict-affected and Fragile Contexts", in: *Issues Paper*, Governance and Social Development Resource Center, GSDRC Issues Paper (Birmingham UK: Governance and Social Development Resource Centre [GSDRC]): 1–42.
Hansen, Annika S., 2008: "Local Ownership in Peace Operations", in: Donais, Timothy (Ed.): *Local Ownership and Security Sector Reform* (Berlin: Lit Verlag).
Hughes, Caroline; Pupavac, Vanessa, 2005: "Framing Post-conflict Societies: international pathologisation of Cambodia and the post-Yugoslav states", in: *Third World Quarterly*, 26, 6: 873–889.
Informal Discussion #23, 2011: Government Agency Representative 23_ID_Ki_III_Ee. Kinshasa.
Interview #2, 2011: Professor 2_JLB_Bu_III_Bb. Ituri.
Interview #4, 2011: Local NGO Representative 4_JMB_Bu_III_Ca. Ituri.
Interview #5, 2011: Local NGO Representative 5_DD_Bu_III_Ca. Ituri.
Interview #8, 2011: Local NGO Representative 8_JM_Bu_III_Ca. Ituri.
Interview #10, 2011: UN Representative (National Staff) 10_JML_Bu_III_Eb. Ituri.
Interview #11, 2011: UN Representative (International Staff) 11_JFD_Bu_III_Ea. Ituri.
Interview #12, 2011: UN Representative (National Staff) 12_PM_Bu_III_Eb. Ituri.
Interview #15, 2011: Church Representative 15_ANB_Bu_III_Cb. Ituri.
Interview #17, 2011: Local NGO Representative 17_PMF_Bu_III_Ca. Ituri.
Interview #21, 2011: Local NGO Representative 21_DL_Mah_III_Ca. Ituri.
Interview #26, 2012: Senior Researcher 26_DT_O_IV_A. Phone Conversation.
Interview #82, 2012: District Authority 82_M_Bu_IV_Bc. Ituri.
Interview #95, 2012: UN Representative (National Staff) 95_JFA_Bu_IV_Eb. Ituri.
Interviews and Focus Group Discussions, Spring 2011/12: Ituri and Kinshasa.
Jarstad, Anna; Olsson, Louise, 2011: "Who Owns What and How? The International and the Local in the Ownership of Security and Development", Paper for the International Studies Association Annual Conference 'Global Governance: Political Authority in Transition', Montreal, Canada, 16 March 2011.

Joseph, Edward P., 2007: "Ownership Is Over-Rated", in: *SAIS Review*, 27, 2: 109–123.

Kang, Sŏng-ho; McDonald, John W.; Pae, Chin-su; Chaedan, Tongbuga Yŏksa, 2009: *Conflict resolution and peacebuilding: the role of NGOs in historical reconciliation and territorial issues* (Seoul, Korea: Northeast Asian History Foundation).

Kuehne, Winrich; Pietz, Tobias; von Carlowitz, Leopold, 2008: "Peacebuilding Processes in Failed States—How to Improve Local Ownership?", Paper for the 49th Annual International Studies Association Convention, San Francisco, 29 March 2008.

Lidén, Kristoffer, 2005: *Whose Peace? Which Peace? On the Political Architecture of Liberal Peacebuilding* (Oslo: PRIO - International Peace Research Institute).

Mac Ginty, Roger, 2008: "Indigenous Peace-Making Versus the Liberal Peace", in: *Cooperation and Conflict: Journal of the Nordic International Studies Association*, 43, 2: 139–163.

Marenin, Otwin, 2005: "Restoring Policing Systems in Conflict Torn Nations: Process, Problems, Prospects", in: *DCAF Occasional Paper, 7*: 1–103.

McCandless, Erin; Abu-Nimer, Mohammed, 2006: "National Ownership in Security, Peacebuilding and Development: Grassroots Activism, Institution Building and Policy Making", in: *Journal of Peacebuilding & Development*, 2, 3: 1–6.

Natsios, Andrew S., 1995: "NGOs and the UN system in complex humanitarian emergencies: conflict or cooperation?", in: *Third World Quarterly*, 16, 3: 405–419.

Newman, Edward; Paris, Roland; Richmond, Oliver, 2009: *New perspectives on liberal peacebuilding* (New York: United Nations University Press).

Paris, Roland; Sisk, Timothy, 2007: "Managing Contradictions: The Inherent Dilemmas of Postwar Statebuilding", in: *IPA Publications* (New York: International Peace Academy).

Pietz, Tobias; von Carlowitz, Leopold, 2007: "Local Ownership in Peacebuilding Processes in Failed States. Approaches, Experiences, and Prerequisites for Success", Paper for the Expert Meeting of the Center for International Peace Operations (ZIF), Berlin, 20–21 April 2007.

Pouligny, Béatrice, 2005: "Civil Society and Post-Conflict Peacebuilding: Ambiguities of International Programmes Aimed at Building 'New' Societies", in: *Security Dialogue*, 36, 4: 495–510.

Pouligny, Béatrice, 2009: "Local Ownership", in: Vincent Chetail *(Ed.): Post-Conflict Peacebuilding. A Lexicon* (Oxford: Oxford University Press): 174–187.

Prendergast, John; Plumb, Emily, 2002: "Building Local Capacity: From Implementation to Peacebuilding", in: Stedman, S. J.; Rothchild, Donald; Cousens, Elizabeth M. (Ed.): *Ending Civil Wars: The Implementation of Peace Agreements* (Boulder, CO: Lynne Rienner Publishers): 327–349.

Ramsbotham, Oliver; Woodhouse, Tom; Miall, Hugh, 2005: *Contemporary Conflict Resolution* (Cambridge: Polity Press).

Reich, Hannah, 2006: *Local Ownership in Conflict Transformation Projects: Partnership, Participation or Patronage?", Berghof Occasional Paper* (Berlin: Berghof Research Center for Constructive Conflict Management): 1–41.

Ricigliano, Robert, 2003: "Networks of effective action: Implementing an integrated approach to peacebuilding", in: *Security Dialogue*, 34, 4: 445–462.

Rogier, Emeric, 2004: "The Inter-Congolese Dialogue: A Critical Overview", in: Malan, Mark; Porto, João Gomes (Ed.): *Challenges of Peace Implementation: The UN Mission in the Democratic Republic of Congo* (Pretoria: Institute for Security Studies): 25–42.

Saxby, John, 2003: *Local ownership and development co-operation - the role of Northern civil society* (Ontario: Canadian Council for International Co-operation Resource Document).

Scheye, Eric; Peake, Gordon, 2005: "Unknotting Local Ownership", in: Ebnöther, Anja H.; Fluri, Philipp H. (Ed.): *After Intervention: Public Security Management in Post-Conflict Societies — From Intervention to Sustainable Local Ownership* (Vienna: Bureau for Security Policy at the Austrian Ministry of Defence; National Defence Academy, Vienna and Geneva Centre for the Democratic Control of Armed Forces, Geneva): 235–260.

Sending, Ole Jacob, 2009: "Why Peacebuilders Fail to Secure Ownership and be Sensitive to Context", in: *Security in Practice* (Norwegian Institute of International Affairs—Department of Security and Conflict Management).

Sending, Ole Jacob, 2010: "Learning to Build a Sustainable Peace: Ownership and Everyday Peacebuilding", in: CMI (Ed.): *Report* (Oslo: CMI).
Smith, Dan, 2004: *Towards a Strategic Framework for Peacebuilding: Getting Their Act Together* (Oslo: PRIO - International Peace Research Institute).
Suhrke, Astrid, 2007: "Reconstruction as Modernisation: The 'Post-Conflict' Project in Afghanistan", in: *Third World Quarterly*, 28, 7: 1291–1308.
van Brabant, Koenraad, 2010: *Peacebuilding How? Broad Local Ownership* (Geneva: Interpeace).
van Tongeren, Paul, 1999: *People building peace : 35 inspiring stories from around the world* (Utrecht: European Centre for Conflict Prevention).
van Tongeren, Paul, 2005: *People building peace II: successful stories of civil society* (Boulder: Lynne Rienner).
von Billerbeck, Sarah B.K., 2011: "Whose Peace? Local Ownership and UN Peacebuilding", in: *Journal of Intervention and Statebuilding*, Special Issue: 322–365.
Woodward, Susan, 2006: "Peacebuilding and 'failed states': some initial considerations", in: Pureza, Manuel José; Duffield, Marc; Matthews, Robert; Woodward, Susan; Sogge, David (Eds.): *Peacebuilding and Failed States: Some Theoretical Notes* (Oficina do CES): 22–28.
Zimmermann, Felix, 2007: *Ownership in Practice*, Paper read at Ownership in Practice, Sèvres, 27–28 September 2007.

Participants at a seminar on social cohesion, Bunia, DR Congo. *Source* Sara Hellmüller/swisspeace. The permission to reproduce this photo was granted.

Chapter 2
Local Ownership and the Settlement of Civil Wars: External Intervention in Internal Armed Conflicts—Arguments for a Conceptual Framework of 'Political Ownership'

Peter Schumann

Abstract Local ownership as currently pursued by external actors may facilitate early recovery and reconstruction in the aftermath of war, but it has little relevance for the durable settlement of civil war. Ownership assumes a different quality and substance when the objective is to achieve a lasting political settlement of civil war, ownership should therefore be operationalized as part of the political process of conflict transformation, and it should be approached as *political ownership*. Political ownership determines not only the quality of the relationship between the conflict parties; it also governs external relations, in particular with those external forces playing a direct role in the peace process. This applies in particular when sovereignty is challenged through externally driven policies, such as the protection of civilians from internal threats or the objection to non-democratic regime change. An externally supported peace process takes place in the context of a tripartite asymmetric relationship. This leads to a very distinct and also uneven division of roles and responsibilities. However, it is argued that a framework conceptualizing political ownership and the lasting settlement of civil war must be part of a comprehensive model to explain the failure of political processes to end civil war.

Keywords Development and ownership · Intra-state conflict and external intervention · Political ownership and durable settlement of civil war · UN Peacekeeping

---

P. Schumann (✉)
Berlin, Germany
e-mail: schumannp@t-online.de

S. Hellmüller and M. Santschi (eds.), *Is Local Beautiful?*,
SpringerBriefs in Environment, Security, Development and Peace 11,
DOI: 10.1007/978-3-319-00306-1_2,

2.1 Introduction[1]

Local ownership refers to an approach advocated in the framework of development cooperation. The assumption is that socio-economic change supported by external aid should not be imposed, it is more sustainable when those affected accept and internalize 'ownership' of the process of innovation as well as the outcome achieved. Ownership is based on principles of partnership, respect, trust and the motivation to achieve common goals.

Any form of external intervention in an intra-state armed conflict is based on different policies and operational procedures and addresses different issues. Civil wars are either settled through military victory of one of the conflict parties or through a negotiated settlement to stop war activities and an agreed political transformation of the conflict. The other option is the open-ended unsettled civil war, which has during recent decades been the most prevalent situation.

In the case of a military victory a regime change or regime consolidation is the likely outcome, with winners and losers as well as victims exposed to atrocities and persecution. The likelihood that armed struggle will resume within a few years is very high. At the core of a negotiated political settlement is a power-sharing arrangement, in addition to other protocols, such as security and wealth sharing arrangements. The situation is totally different when conflict is prolonged. Low intensity internal strife and sudden eruption of deadly fighting take place more or less at random and governments remain in power as a result of the ongoing crisis. External intervention takes place as a parallel event with marginal effects on the deadly crisis.

The issue under review is the role of 'ownership' in the process to transform a violent armed conflict into a process of non-violent political change, a peace process. Looking in detail at the role of an external intervention in the process to influence or resolve internal armed struggle and civil war, be it through UN peacekeeping operations (UNPKO) or hybrid arrangements, the results achieved are so far not convincing, neither from a security or protection point of view nor from a political perspective of conflict transformation. There is evidence which suggests that the failure of external intervention seems to be related to 'ownership' or the simple question 'whose peace is it?'.

External actors operating within the framework of a UNPKO perform functions as observers and monitors, they report on compliance and facilitate processes through 'good office functions', in addition, they perform logistics and operational support functions. Principles of partnership and sustainability as core elements of 'local ownership' may play a role in the case of activities supported by external actors outside the political dimension of a peace process, by far the largest part of a PKO, but at the same time the least important for resolving conflict. Activities

[1] This chapter was presented at the swisspeace annual conference 2012. I am grateful to the organizers for the opportunity to present and debate issues discussed in this chapter, in particular to Sara Hellmüller.

directly related to the peace process take place in a complex political and fragile security environment. External participation in these core activities is limited, often rejected as a result of lack of trust, fundamental disagreement with external advice and outright rejection of demands to conform with standards set by representatives of the international community. This chapter argues that local ownership as currently pursued by external actors may facilitate early recovery and reconstruction, but it has little relevance for the durable settlement of civil war and civil strive. It draws attention to the political dimension of the peace process and argues that 'political ownership' needs to be given a prominent role, in particular when external actors intend to play a role in making peace. This implies a need to accept that the conflict parties are in the driver's seat, not the external actors.

2.2 Background

The issue under review appears to be rather straightforward. When political systems collapse and governments are under imminent threat, when armed uprisings and rebel movements gain international attention, when large scale displacement affects major parts of the population and humanitarian operations are launched to save people's lives and when the overall political situation is considered a threat to international peace and stability, an external intervention is considered the only option. Under these conditions the UN Security Council will authorize a PKO. Based on the consent of the government and the officially recognized rebel movement an international intervention is organized, mandated to support the parties of the conflict to reach a negotiated settlement and to provide assistance to rebuild a war torn society, establish systems of rule of law and build state institutions in line with UN policy principles and standards of governance.

Peacekeeping tasks authorized by the UN Security Council are funded through assessed contributions of member states to the UN peacekeeping budget. Any additional activities are initiated through bilateral assistance, funded by voluntary contributions from donor governments. Irrespective of the source of funding, the principle applies that all activities and programmes are planned and implemented first of all in cooperation with, and with the consent of, the government, including under certain conditions 'rebel movements' and institutions established as a result of a peace agreement.[2]

'Local ownership', in the context of development cooperation has become a normative element governing external intervention, put into practice through different means such as 'consent', 'participation' or 'joint partnerships'. This chapter argues that a negotiated cessation of armed hostilities and an

[2] This is in particular the case when a 'comprehensive peace agreement' was signed and interim arrangements are put in place until a final government is formed, for example through elections. See Sudan Comprehensive Peace Agreement, at: http://unmis.unmissions.org/Portals/UNMIS/Documents/General/cpa-en.pdf (5 June 2013).

understanding on political principles signed by the conflict parties in the form of post-war power-security-and wealth sharing protocols has more to do with undemocratic re-arranging of internal power structures, including the option of forced 'regime change', than the achievement of socio-economic, governance and environmental development goals. The process of advancing from a formalized negotiated agreement to a political settlement of an armed conflict normally takes years. At the end, a new compact will have emerged between the political elite of military leaders and the elected representatives on the one hand and civil society, including the tolerated political opposition, on the other hand. The political dimension of 'local ownership' has a different quality and substance when the objective is to achieve a 'durable political settlement of civil war' which always includes the option to apply military and other enforcement action (Duffy Toft 2010).

However, there is yet another dimension of 'local ownership', viewed from the perspective of the conflict parties and, as the process advances, the new government. 'Local ownership' has first of all a lot to do with the quality of the relationship between conflict parties. In addition, it defines the policy principles and operational arrangements of external relationship with UN member state governments in general and donor governments in particular. 'Local ownership' in the context of a fragile state or a civil war affected nation has during the past decade become an element of international relations, i.e. the targeted intervention in an internal conflict has become an element of foreign policy.

The Government of the Republic of South Sudan has perceived the mandate of the UN Mission in the Republic of South Sudan (UNMISS), approved by the UN Security Council under Chapter VII of the UN Charter, as an interference in the internal affairs of the newly independent sovereign nation state, resulting in rather constrained relations with UNMISS leadership and the UN Secretary General. The political dimension of 'local ownership' has become a key element describing the relationship between the UN and member states. The UN Secretary General points out that "no … reform imposed from outside can hope to be successful or sustainable" and continues that the UN "must learn better how to respect and support local ownership, local leadership and local constituency of reform, while at the same time remaining faithful to UN norms and standards".[3] As von Carlowitz (2011: 6) concludes, "while policy-makers, academics and practitioners generally agree with these statements in theory, local ownership proves difficult to operationalize in post-conflict assistance and governance, and remains mere rhetoric in many international reform programmes".

The underlying issue is the following: under UN peacekeeping policies and rules the international community intervening in the framework of a UN Security Council authorized peacekeeping operation, implemented in cooperation with regional organizations and further supported through bilateral programmes of

[3] UN Report of the Secretary General, The rule of law and transitional justice in conflict and post-conflict societies, UN Doc. S/2004/616, 3 August 2004, para 17.

interested governments, accepts cooperation with the conflict parties, comprising of the member state government, rebels and others, and to support policies and operational activities in the context of conflict resolution and ending civil war. These programmes are, as a matter of principle, to be formulated jointly with those who have come to power through armed struggle or retained some form of residual government authority, which in any case implies violation of human rights and large scale atrocities committed against the civilian population. These programmes may in the end pursue policies not in the immediate interest of individual member states. The principle of cooperation aims to achieve 'ownership' and implies that external actors and local leadership share common objectives and cooperate in the implementation of programmes and projects.[4] The principle of cooperation, however, seems to be a moving target. The Peacebuilding Commission, for instance, "shall work in cooperation with national or transitional authorities, where possible, in the country under consideration with a view to ensuring national ownership of the peacebuilding process".[5] The resolution does not prevent the Commission from initiating activities where cooperation on the part of the government or transitional authority is not forthcoming.

In view of the frequent break-down of agreements followed by the resumption of armed confrontation and the systemic failure of UN peace operations to ensure that agreements are honoured, the principle of 'local ownership' as an underlying principle of cooperation needs careful analysis and review. It seems that most of the debates to explain failure of peace agreements and the resumption of war activities focus on operational activities and the implications of 'lack of ownership'. These explanations are very similar to those given to explain the failure of development cooperation programmes to reduce poverty or enhance public health or other dimensions of the millennium development goals. This seems to be in particular the case when negotiated agreements are of a tactical nature and not the result of a comprehensive political process or in situations where external pressure was the main driver for the parties of the conflict to negotiate an initial agreement.

The process to end civil war and to implement post-war nation building programmes and foster regime change is part of complex political arrangements, which include elements such as constitutional reform, sharing of power, elections and universal application of rights ensuring that all groups of society, irrespective of religion, ethnic origin or other criteria of discrimination, are protected and enjoy safety and security.

External interventions are part and parcel of this process and principles of cooperation and best practices should be applied, including 'local ownership'. Security Council decisions mandating a peace operation make explicit reference to the role of member state governments; they describe in detail the responsibilities of the peacekeeping operation and demand cooperation from the government as

---

[4] UN General Assembly, Peacebuilding in the aftermath of conflict, A/67/499, 8 October 2012.

[5] UN Security Council, Resolution on the establishment of the Peacebuilding Commission, S/RES/1645, 12 December 2005, para 10.

well as rebel movements concerned.[6] With the role political institutions such as the UN Security Council as well as regional organizations (AU) play in the process to authorize, plan and implement external interventions to end civil war, 'local ownership' as understood in the context of development cooperation as 'joint' and 'participatory' would be intentionally misleading, in particular when Chapter VII of the UN Charter is invoked.

The underlying principles of external intervention, ranging from 'sustaining war' to 'achieving durable peace' and addressing the causes of political dissent and armed opposition as well as the 'intended failure' of state institutions to protect civilian population under imminent threat, go beyond 'local ownership' as described earlier. In addition to the expansion of 'operational activities' there is a proliferation of global policy goals which may have little to do with the causes of the conflict but which derive from international norm setting processes, for example as the outcome of UN global conferences and which are, as a matter of principle, included in the mandate of peace operations.[7] UN peace operations have become instruments for achieving compliance with these norms, the extent of 'local ownership' is used to determine the level of compliance, measured through the incorporation of these norms, for example in national legislation. Peacekeeping is used as a means of broadening the political agenda of the external intervention, often losing sight of those issues central to the transformation of a violent conflict.

Local ownership in the development cooperation domain remains focused on issues of aid effectiveness and to what extent development assistance should align itself with local systems and practices. Donor practices are adapting and policy and political conditionality are re-emerging. However, at the same time attention is drawn to the need to respect national sovereignty. It is acknowledged that there are non-aid issues in development and that a different concept of what development cooperation is about may be required (Booth 2011: 4).

In view of the conceptual and operational limitations described so far, it is argued that local ownership and external intervention as currently advocated and applied has limited relevance in the political process to settle civil war through a negotiated agreement.[8] However, there is also another very important observation, drawing attention to the exclusive responsibility of local politics to end armed conflict. The responsibility to launch armed struggle is predominantly a domestic affair and is based on a range of often very complex decisions. The same principle applies to end the armed struggle, it is a process which must be politically owned by local leadership and find broad based acceptance.

---

[6] Security Council Resolution, S/RES/1590, 24 March 2005; Security Council Resolution, S/RES/1996, 8 July 2011; Security Council Resolution, S/RES/2046, 2 May 2012 "decides that Sudan and South Sudan shall take the following actions with immediate effect" following the resumption of armed conflict between the Republics of South Sudan and Sudan.

[7] The opening paragraphs of Security Council decisions authorizing Peacekeeping Operations refer to all relevant UN General Assembly and UN Security Council decisions without establishing a specific relevance with the country concerned.

[8] Local ownership in the case of military victory to end civil war needs to be explored separately.

The prolonged political crisis in Somalia is a case in point. The reconciliation and peace conferences as well as the establishment of the Transitional Federal Government (TFG) are externally initiated, donor financed processes, politically controlled by regional and international actors, and so far without tangible results. On the other hand, the establishment of the government and public administration in Somaliland are locally driven and have so far neither received international recognition nor political support. They are exclusively accountable to local actors, represented by clan elders, organizations of youth, women, and professionals, such as lawyers, medical doctors and businessmen. Political processes are first of all locally driven events, where the acknowledgement of locally dictated conditions defines what is possible (Hirsi 2011). Therefore, 'ownership' seems to be first of all a function of political representation and organization, accountability and legitimacy based on cultural norms and practices and external relations based on respect for sovereignty, international norms and standards, for example of governance and nation-building which are accepted as distant goals.

2.3 Assumptions and Myths: Towards a Political Approach to 'Local Ownership' in an Asymmetric Tripartite Relationship

As argued above, policies and operational procedures of external interventions to end armed conflict and civil war have little in common with development cooperation programmes. Still, the assumption persists that instruments, procedures and experiences from development cooperation are applicable to situations of 'war and peace'. The application of development based needs assessment and programme formulation processes leads to the interpretation of the causes of conflict and the dynamics of conflict conversion as deep rooted development deficits. These similarities at first sight result in confusion about cause and effect and exclude a deeper look at the political causes of dissent, armed opposition and war.[9]

The underlying causes which lead people to take up arms may result in political demands which relate to underdevelopment and deprivation, in particular when targeted deprivation and intended underdevelopment are part of government policies to deal with specific population groups or regions in opposition to the central government. However, the process of moving from political opposition to dissent and armed struggle is a complex one and may differ from case to case. The struggle for independence against a colonial power follows a different political and military pattern than the fight of a particular ethnic or religious community against the central government's policies resulting in marginalization and oppression. The

[9] The correlation between underdevelopment and internal armed struggle lacks empirical evidence. Still, it is frequently used as argument to justify the submission of reconstruction and development appeals at donor pledging conferences, justified as part of the peace process.

likelihood of reaching a durable negotiated settlement of a conflict depends therefore to a large extent on the political demands and the military evolution of the struggle. Negotiated settlements fail because they neither address these demands nor do they acknowledge during the implementation process the difference between a negotiated peace agreement and the lasting settlement of a conflict. "Providing external support to a political settlement is therefore a deeply political undertaking. Yet, so are the challenges facing outside actors with regards to peacebuilding and statebuilding in the first place. Addressing these challenges with concepts that help grasp the full complexity of the task at hand is necessary for any sustainable success" (OECD 2011: 13).

The limited knowledge and empirical analysis about the specific causes of an armed conflict, the principles of war fighting and methods of destabilization and the political options of conflict transformation are factors which have resulted in a template approach of external intervention through UNPKOs.

The UN Security Council mandates PKOs to perform functions which provide support; only in exceptional cases do PKOs perform executive functions, which require specific authorization under Chapter VII of the UN Charter. Government, rebel movements and others covered under the mandate retain full responsibility, for example for the implementation of jointly signed agreements. This is an officially acknowledged recognition of 'ownership', it assigns political responsibility. One would therefore expect that UNPKOs have over time developed a variety of methods to operationalize support and local ownership, based on best practices derived from different peacekeeping scenarios.

However, reality seems to be different when it comes to clarity about operational roles and responsibilities. The regular reports of the UN Secretary General to the UN Security Council about the implementation of the mandate record progress made, describe the status of affairs to address highly complex issues, such as the protection of civilians from attacks of regular and rebel forces, support of democratization and rule of law at different levels of government, providing good offices in case of complex political negotiations and offering technical solutions to reform post war security apparatus, to mention the most common functions.

These reports are prepared by the mission leadership and the office of the Secretary General; they do not include inputs from the conflict parties as they are reviews of their performance and compliance with the provisions of the mandate. In particular governments but also 'transitional administrations' or others referred to in the mandate object to any form of criticism and seek their own ways and means to demonstrate that they have the option to act independently from the PKO and the Security Council. They may simply try to take advantage of the logistical support capacities of PKOs or request the performance of specific tasks, also in pursuit of their own political goals. The relationship between the conflict parties and the UNPKO can best be characterized as an asymmetric tripartite constellation; neither based on equal partnership nor jointly agreed rules. This discrepancy about the expected and de facto role of a UNPKO leads to the notion of interference in internal affairs, where ownership becomes a matter of competition and contradiction, in particular when it is used to attribute responsibility for the failure of local actors to comply with the mandate of the mission. Ownership is therefore a function of political power of each actor in a tripartite relationship and the political goals and objectives pursued by each of these actors.

2.4 Ownership in the Context of Norms and Practices of the International Community: The Clash of Policy Intentions and Organizational Realities in the Context of UN Peacekeeping Operations

Interventions of external actors in a country considered a threat to international security due to internal armed struggle are politically controversial, operationally complex and subject to intensive media scrutiny. UN member states participating in these operations have to provide their own 'home audience' with plausible explanations to justify both possible positions of intervention and abstention. Intended outcomes of the operation and questions of legitimacy, legality and global responsibilities are asked, in particular in settings of liberal democracies and active civil society organizations raising their voices on behalf of war affected civilian populations under imminent threat.[10]

'Ownership' in the context of an intervention in an internal violent conflict seems to be more of an illusion than a reality, in particular when sovereignty is understood as a political responsibility to continue the 'liberation struggle'. This is an emerging reality in South Sudan, where the leadership has left no doubt over its perception of sovereignty and ownership when external actors lost control over the political process in May 2012 and the breakdown of mediation efforts of the African Union (AU) High Implementation Panel and a resumption of armed hostilities between South Sudan and Sudan.

Mandates authorizing peace operations are the result of complex political negotiations between members of the UN Security Council reflecting their own security policy concerns and other interests, in addition to those of the conflict parties. In order to achieve a majority vote in particular of the P-5, mandates may lack policy clarity, provide room for operational ambiguities and prescribe measures unrelated to the conflict (Seibel 2011: 271–287).

The reform of peacekeeping[11] and the development of international norms and policies of external intervention have strengthened the institutional framework of peacekeeping (Deng 1996; Annan 2005). However, the stated goals of UN

[10] The moral dilemma that each intervention which did not take place is as problematic as the one which has taken place is of much debate in particular in the context of "The Responsibility to Protect" (ICISS Report; at: http://responsibilitytoprotect.org/ICISS%20Report.pdf (5 June 2013)).

[11] Brahimi Report 2000; at: www.un.org/peace/reports/peace_operations (5 June 2013), in particular Chapter VI. The Brahimi Report does not address the issue of 'local ownership'.

peacekeeping reform programmes and the progress reported regularly by the UN Secretary General to the UN General Assembly and the UN Security Council have only limited impact on the durable political settlement of conflict in particular in the most notorious conflict zones, such as the wider region of the Horn of Africa.

The failure of these reform programmes to trickle down to the war affected countries and to strengthen peace operations seems to depend on the role of local institutions and the responsibilities of the new post-war political leadership.

2.4.1 The First Paradox: The Making of a PKO—Planned Absence of Ownership

UNPKOs are planned according to a well-defined and established integrated planning process, with the intention to bring all relevant UN and other external actors together. Operational realities on the ground are assessed through visits to the conflict zone, at least to those areas considered safe and for which the government grants access.

Local actors are neither included in the decision making part of the planning process, nor do they have an active role in the implementation. The Special Representative of the Secretary General (SRSG) reports as mandated in the resolution on the implementation of the peace operation, this report is a UN document. Therefore, the formulation takes place without inputs from the conflict parties. The UN peacekeeping planning bureaucracy is in the lead, guided by processes to keep the peace within the UN system and in line with UN global policy goals. The final political decision to approve the operation remains with the UN Security Council while budgetary decisions are approved by the UN General Assembly on recommendation of the Budgetary Committee of the UN. Peacekeeping principles such as 'consent of the conflict parties' to the external intervention are adhered to during the initial planning and approval process, but the approval of subsequent periodic renewal of the operation neither requires consent nor is it subject to an independent evaluation of the results achieved. The making of a PKO assumes 'local ownership', but it does not provide for it.

2.4.2 The Second Paradox: The Implementation of Operational Activities—Intended Neglect of Ownership

Following the approval of a UN peacekeeping operation, implementation at the country level takes place under the overall leadership of the SRSG. At the operational level the PKO needs the cooperation and, in a number of instances, the formal approval of the government to establish the mission and to ensure that activities can be implemented. Practical experience, for example in the case of the UN Mission in Sudan (UNMIS) but also the UN Mission in Darfur (UNAMID) has demonstrated that operational activities of both missions were severely affected by the lack of administrative, security and logistics approvals by the Government of Sudan.

While the planning of peacekeeping operations takes place under the nearly exclusive authority of the UN and selected member states (groups of friends), the implementation depends to a large extent on political decisions governing administrative support of the host government as well as rebel movements or transitional authorities in areas under their control.

External actors, such as donor governments supporting specific elements of a PKO with their own resources, require host government approval to implement programmes, even in instances of humanitarian assistance in support of a war affected civilian population.

The implementation of operational activities mandated in a UN Security Council Resolution may take place successfully, however this does not imply that conflict origins are addressed or that threat levels affecting a civilian population are reduced or effectively controlled.

2.4.3 The Third Paradox: UN Peacekeeping Principles—Sovereign Ownership

UN peacekeeping principles are directly related to the principle adherence to and protection of the sovereignty of UN member states (Bellamy et al. 2004). Any interference in the internal affairs of a UN member state requires the consent of the government concerned. The implementation of the UN policy on the protection of civilians under imminent threat or the adherence to the UN approved policy on the 'Responsibility to Protect' requires as a matter of principle host government approval. 'Local ownership' as a policy can only be implemented within the overall principle of sovereignty.

Local ownership as an operational principle to implement activities in support of peace operations is faced with a dilemma. While operations are planned and approved outside the authority of the government affected, implementation is governed by principles under the control of the sovereign member state or rebel movements exercising territorial control. Member states even affected by conflict exercise in fact 'political ownership' and therefore determine to a large extent the outcome of the external intervention.

Peacekeeping principles strengthen the political capacity of governments under imminent threat, they facilitate the application of peacekeeping operations for the achievement of their own political goals, including military objectives against rebel forces.[12] However, there are exceptions, such as the multi-dimensional PKO in Kosovo (UNMIK) when the Government of Serbia was denied the authority to continue to govern the province under the executive mandate of UNMIK, authorized by the UN Security Council to operate under Chapter VII of the UN Charter. 'Local ownership' became a synonym for 'interim transitional administration' with the local self-government authorized to perform 'transferred functions of government' under international supervision and control.

2.5 Towards a Conceptual Framework of 'Political Ownership' and the Lasting Settlement of Civil War

This paper has argued that political ownership is a major element of an overall conceptual framework for a lasting settlement of civil war. The case was made that local ownership has a justification as a normative requirement in a sustainable development cooperation programme and that external intervention in civil war and civil strife do require a different approach in order to address the complex political situation of war and peace. Political ownership was defined in the context of an asymmetric tripartite relationship between conflict parties, normally the government and rebel movements, and a peacekeeping operation authorized by the UN Security Council.

Political ownership as part of a tripartite arrangement will be determined by the following issues:

1. The origins and dynamics of the armed struggle and intended as well as already realized political demands will define the overall framework of conflict transformation.

External interventions may promote solutions which often ignore the findings of a substantive conflict analysis and do not evaluate options to end the conflict. External interveners perceive conflicts from a different perspective than that of local actors and tend to prescribe short term solutions. The implications of this approach are substantial. At the political level they may lead to the resumption of war while at the operational level activities are implemented which are unrelated to the conflict.

Conflict resolution activities should be based on conflict parameters and the political ownership of the process of conflict transformation must remain with the conflict parties. External actors must limit their intervention to operational

[12] The acceptance of the demand of the Government of Sudan that the character of UNAMID must be "African" limited the options of the UN Secretary General to staff the mission, in particular at the senior level. The bargaining power of the Government of Sudan was further strengthened when DPKO and the Secretary General accepted without protest the dismissal of the SRSG Jan Pronk in October 2006.

activities of conflict transformation. This includes mediation and other negotiation support activities on request by the conflict parties.

2. There is more than one option to end political rebellion and armed conflict, all must be considered, irrespective of political and other priorities external actors may pursue. This includes military victory of either party to the conflict, negotiated agreements in response to political demands to end all or partial war activities as well as reaching a new social and political contract to rebuild society.

External interventions play very different roles and perform a range of functions during the different phases of an internal armed conflict, depending primarily on the options pursued by the conflict parties. The objective of the conflict parties is to make use of the external intervention in pursuit of their own political and military goals. This includes humanitarian assistance. Historical data shows that the durable settlement of civil war depends only marginally on external intervention. The more promising option is an internally negotiated solution guaranteed by external powers. However, external powers only rarely provide credible guarantees, and only in very few instances have these guarantees been invoked following the breach of an agreement (Duffy Toft 2010: 30–32).[13] The lack of empirical data limits the formulation of a theoretical model explaining the options to end civil war and the probability of success.

3. Agreements are negotiated to first and foremost end ongoing armed struggle and civil war, followed by political negotiations to reach an understanding on political principles for a political settlement. As agreements are implemented, political negotiations must continue to address unresolved issues. The role of external actors is primarily to guarantee the implementation of agreements and be prepared to sanction non-compliance in line with agreed mechanisms and activities. Opportunities for intended failure and launching of new armed struggle when political arrangements fail must be considered at all times.

The civil war in Sudan is characterized by "dishonoured agreements" (Alier 1990), external failure to sanction the systematic breach of agreements and international actors primarily guided by a variety of interests more in line with their own foreign policy goals (Schumann 2010: 102–14). Instead external actors have demonstrated nearly unlimited support for never ending negotiation processes. Local leadership has taken advantage of this situation and used negotiations as an opportunity to overcome military disadvantages or to strengthen negotiation positions. The failure to implement strategic elements of the Comprehensive Peace Agreement (2005) and the endorsement of this selective approach by the international community can be considered as a key element in

[13] She draws attention to the role external actors should play to stabilize peace agreements and political settlements.

explaining the resumption of armed aggression between the two newly created Republics.

In addition to these political process issues, a conceptual framework for the lasting settlement of civil war must be framed under consideration of the following realities emerging as a result of ongoing and past peace processes and to a large extent independent of the actual conflict scenario.

Peace agreements negotiated with external mediation assistance have resulted in increasingly complex legal documents with detailed implementation arrangements. These so called 'comprehensive peace agreements' follow a standard pattern, with security arrangements, power and wealth sharing agreements as well as special protocols. They also include a mechanism to assess and evaluate the implementation of the agreement.

While the government has the option of involving any entity of the government administration in the negotiation as well as the implementation process, rebel movements are at a disadvantage and must rely on their own capacity or enter into arrangements with external actors offering support. External actors, including UN officials, traditionally maintain the political relationship they had with government representatives before and during the war, and the government continues to represent the country in all official functions and entities of the UN and its member states. The UN depends on the consent of the government for all actions it decides to take, for example the 'status of forces agreement' with the UN. Therefore political ownership remains primarily with the government. This unequal relationship results in an asymmetric peace process.

Little empirical data and analysis are available on the implementation of peace agreements. The only systematic reporting which has been undertaken is part of the framework of reports of the UN Secretary General to the Security Council as per the mandate of a peace operation.

Information about the need to either re-negotiate parts of the agreement or to find an agreement on issues which emerged as a result of the peace agreement is very limited. Early warning about the need to find solutions to unresolved issues is therefore marginal. Still, the implementation of a peace agreement is a dynamic process, with the inherent threat of failure. This situation is further aggravated when there is only limited political ownership of the negotiated solution, for example when the initial assumptions of the peace agreement are no longer valid.[14]

Negotiations taking place under conditions briefly described above tend not to be successful. Unresolved issues emerging as a result of changed assumptions may be re-negotiated outside the peace agreement or form the basis for a new agreement altogether.

[14] This applies to the Comprehensive Peace Agreement (CPA) signed between the Government of the Sudan and the Sudan Peoples Liberation Movement (SPLM). The objective of the CPA was to create conditions for a reformed and "New Sudan", separation was considered then a remote option only.

The most obvious is not the most valid: the role of external interventions in internal armed conflict as an element of conflict transformation and driver of durable peace may be obvious but, there is limited empirical evidence to suggest that current practices of external intervention are in fact strategic drivers of peace.

It should be remembered that processes and instruments applied in UN peace operations in internal armed conflicts originate from situations of inter-state wars. Intra-state wars, normally referred to as civil wars or internal armed strife and rebellion, are relatively new for the UN. The rapid growth of UN peacekeeping in internal conflicts should not detract from realities of institutional shortcomings and limitations.

2.6 Conclusions and Observations

Peacekeeping is fraught with examples of frequent policy failures, institutionalized delays, breakdowns of political processes and the breach of agreements reached. Having said that, there is limited empirical investigation and systematic research to explain how civil wars end or why they continue. So far we have little verified knowledge about the ending of civil wars, despite high levels of investment in the particular approach of a negotiated agreement supported by external intervention through a UN Security Council mandated peacekeeping operation. A framework conceptualizing political ownership and the lasting settlement of civil war must be part of a comprehensive theoretical model which should have the capacity to explain the failure of political processes to end civil wars.

Intergovernmental bodies such as the UN and its Department of Peacekeeping Operations (DPKO) have demonstrated that organizational learning takes place. A range of operational policies were improved to make operations more effective, there is field based knowledge about what works and how to avoid failure, and capacity development during the past years has shown results and systems to support operations have improved. However, while the bureaucracy has demonstrated the ability to learn, the political leadership of the UN, in particular of the Security Council and related political organs, does not learn (Seibel 2011). The Security Council continues to authorize peacekeeping operations which do not respond to the causes of the crisis and it continues not to anticipate risks while at the same time encouraging the exploration of political opportunities (Schumann 2012).[15]

[15] The initial recommendations for a peace operation in South Sudan made by UNMIS are in total contrast to the mission approved by the UN Security Council under resolution S/RES/1996 UN Security Council 2011 of 8 July 2011. Neither the Government of the newly independent Republic of South Sudan nor UN Staff with long standing experience in Sudan and South Sudan do agree with the approved mission mandate and concept (Discussions held by the author with the Government of South Sudan and UNMISS officials in March 2011).

The assumed relationship between political ownership and the effectiveness of the external intervention is so far more of a myth than a reflection of reality on the ground. The introduction of 'political ownership' is an attempt to motivate thinking 'outside the box' and to indicate through an overall conceptual framework the complexities of the approach. It is an appeal against yet another simplification of an issue determining the survival of civilian populations under imminent threat and a warning about the limitations of an external intervention to achieve durable and lasting peace. There is a need to draw a red, or in the context of the UN, a blue line and define the limitations of external interventions to end civil war.

References

Alier, Abel, 1990: *Southern Sudan: Too Many Agreements Dishonored* (Oxford: Ithaca Press, Exeter).

Booth, David, 2011: "Aid effectiveness: bringing country ownership (and politics) back in", in: ODI Working Paper, 336.

Brahimi Report, 2000; at: www.un.org/peace/reports/peace_operations (5 June 2013).

Deng, Francis Mading, et al., 1996: *Sovereignty As Responsibility: Conflict Management in Africa* (Washington: Brooking Institution Press).

Duffy Toft, Monica, 2010: *Securing the Peace, the durable settlement of civil war* (Princeton, N.J.: Princeton Univ. Press).

Ferhadbegovic, Sabina; Weiffen, Britta (Eds.), 2011: *Bürgekriege erzählen, Zum Verlauf unziviler Konflikte* (Konstanz: Konstanz University Press).

Hirsi, Ahmed A., 2011: *Political Ownership is it the key to the dispute between Somalis and the international community?*; at: www.hiiraan.com/op2/2011/jun/political_ownership (23 June 2011).

Kofi, Annan, 2005: *In larger freedom: towards development, security and human rights for all*, A/59/2005/Add.1 (New York: United Nations).

OECD, 2011: *From Power Struggles to Sustainable Peace* (Paris: OECD).

Schumann, Peter, 2010: "International Actors in Sudan: The politics of implementing comprehensive peace", in: Heinrich Böll Foundation (Ed.): *Sudan – No easy ways ahead*, Democracy, 18 (Berlin: Heinrich Böll Foundation).

Schumann, Peter, 2012: "Die UN auf dem Prüfstand – warum die Zwei-Staaten-Lösung Südsudan bislang keinen Frieden gebracht hat", in: *Vereinte Nationen*, 60, 3: 106–112.

Seibel, Wolfgang, 2011: "Gewollte Unwissenheit, wenn Friedensorganisationen lernen, Politiker aber nicht" in: Ferhadbegovic, Sabina, Weifen, Britta (Eds.), *Bürgerkriege erzählen, Zum Verlauf unziviler Konflikte* (Konstanz: Konstanz University Press).

UN General Assembly, 2012: *Peacebuilding in the aftermath of conflict*, A/67/499, 8 October 2012 (New York: United Nations).

UN Report of the Secretary General, 2004: *The rule of law and transitional justice in conflict and post-conflict societies*, UN Doc. S/2004/616, 3 August 2004, para 17 (New York: United Nations).

UN Security Council, 2005: Resolution, S/RES/1590, 24 March 2005 (New York: United Nations).

UN Security Council, 2005: *Resolution on the establishment of the Peacebuilding Commission*, S/RES/1645, 12 December 2005, para 10 (New York: United Nations).

UN Security Council 2011: Resolution, S/RES/1996, 8 July 2011 (New York: United Nations).

UN Security Council 2012: Resolution, S/RES/2046, 2 May 2012 (New York: United Nations).

von Carlowitz, Leopold, 2011: "Local ownership in practice: Justice Sector Reform in Kosovo and Liberia", in: DCAF Occasional Papers, 23.

UN airplanes in Entebbe, Uganda. *Source* Sara Hellmüller/swisspeace. Permission to use this photo was granted.

Chapter 3
Shooting Bambi? Critical Reflections on International Approaches to Local Ownership

Marco Pfister

Abstract This chapter critically reflects on the panel on 'International Approaches to Local Ownership' at the swisspeace 2012 annual conference, which featured a representative of a donor institution, the founder and CEO of an international peacebuilding NGO, and a scholar with extensive experience in UN peacekeeping operations. The chapter exposes the nearly insurmountable difficulties that external actors face when trying to implement the concept of local ownership, even when they have the best of intentions. Aside from struggling to define what exactly the term means, they are not able to (or don't want to, and perhaps shouldn't) overcome the power imbalances between donor and target beneficiaries. As the concept of inclusiveness, suggested as an alternative to ownership during the panel, carries similar challenges, the author offers transparency and honesty of external interveners' agendas and intervention approaches as a perhaps more empowering solution that could lead to a more equal partnership between the respective actors.

Keywords Peacebuilding · Local ownership · Inclusiveness · South Sudan · DR Congo

3.1 Introduction

For many years now, 'local ownership' has been a buzzword of the international aid discourse. Faced with the prospect of failing to achieve the Millennium Development Goals, the international community has over the last decade invested an increasing effort in attempting to improve the effectiveness of its assistance. Various global conferences have taken place, and with the 2005 Paris Declaration,

M. Pfister (✉)
swisspeace, Bern, Switzerland
University of Basel, Basel, Switzerland
e-mail: marco.pfister@gmail.com

S. Hellmüller and M. Santschi (eds.), *Is Local Beautiful?*,
SpringerBriefs in Environment, Security, Development and Peace 11,
DOI: 10.1007/978-3-319-00306-1_3,

'ownership' was officially declared one of five 'fundamental principles' of effective aid.[1] The 2011 High Level Forum in Busan confirmed this and emphasized its relevance in fragile contexts in one of the conference outputs, the 'New Deal for Engagement in Fragile States'.[2]

The concept had already found its way much earlier into the arena of international peacebuilding efforts—which in the broadest terms could actually be defined as 'aid in fragile contexts'. Despite the considerable attention accorded to it before and during the drafting of the New Deal, one observer recently noted that "many questions still remain unanswered, especially on how to establish a new relationship between donors and recipient countries but also between governments and their societies" (Chade 2012: 1). Although avoiding the term itself, this quote brings to the fore some of the greatest challenges associated with the implementation of the ideal of local ownership, in particular the problems related to the power imbalances within these relationships. In this context, the 2012 swisspeace annual conference on "Peacebuilding between External Interventions and Locally Led Initiatives" provided a timely platform for critical reflection and debates on these questions. The conference's second panel on "International Approaches to Local Ownership" brought together representatives of three different types of international institutions:

- *Ambassador Claude Wild* spoke in his position as Head of the Human Security Division at the Swiss Federal Department of Foreign Affairs and thus provided a donor perspective,
- *Mr. Peter Schumann* drew on his 30 years of experience in numerous UN peacekeeping missions, including most recently as Regional Coordinator for South Sudan at the United Nations Mission in Sudan, but also spoke in his position as Senior Research Fellow at the University of Konstanz,
- *Mrs. Carolyn Hayman*, Founder and CEO of the UK-based NGO *Peace Direct*, provided a perspective from the non-profit sector, which is generally perceived as being 'closest to the people'. Her organization is particularly attuned to the concept of local ownership, as it writes of itself: "Peace Direct believes in the power of local peacebuilders. We find, fund and promote their work because local people know what's going on in their country".[3]

The present chapter embeds the discussions that took place in this panel in current academic and policy debates and critically reflects on them. It presents the tremendous challenges faced by international peacebuilding actors when attempting to put the concept of local ownership into practice. To this end it takes into consideration the contextual aspects of peacebuilding interventions that differentiate them from development interventions. The chapter argues that in light of the

[1] See http://www.oecd.org/dac/effectiveness/parisdeclarationandaccraagendaforaction.htm (1 April 2013).

[2] See http://www.newdeal4peace.org/ (1 April 2013).

[3] See the Peace Direct website at http://www.newdeal4peace.org/ (1 April 2013).

almost insurmountable obstacles, a shift of attention toward another principle of assistance, *inclusiveness*, may be more conducive to increased effectiveness. It concludes by considering outsider *honesty* as perhaps an even better alternative.

3.2 Semantic and Operational Challenges

Any external intervention intending to secure local ownership faces the problem of defining and identifying the 'local'. Even though most often the term is equated with 'domestic' (as opposed to foreign), one could also emphasize the difference between the local and the national, or between 'simple' citizens or the 'grassroots' and powerful elites and governments (see e.g. Autesserre 2010: 247). The list of dichotomies can be extended at will. But even if consensus is found on the meaning of the term, the probably most significant challenge related to the concept of local ownership remains present: that the 'local' is not homogeneous, whether at the national or at the local level, or among the elites or the population as a whole (see MacGinty 2011: 51). The relevance of this challenge is particularly acute in peacebuilding, which by its very nature takes place in contexts where different views and priorities of local parties have appeared so irreconcilable that they resorted to pursuing them by violent means.

How panel participants identified their 'local' counterparts is telling in this regard but also highlights the need to differentiate between different types of interventions, or at least different approaches. Wild, whose institution is often directly involved in the mediation of peace agreements, defined 'local' actors as those who are *affected* by a particular conflict (and the corresponding peacebuilding intervention) (see Reich 2006: 21 for a similar definition). While this does not solve the semantic problem at hand but rather creates a new one of defining what it means to be affected, such a criterion does indeed appear more relevant than a geographic one.

Wild also strongly emphasized the need to engage with all actors that have the potential to *influence* processes, be it positively or negatively. One could argue that this marginalizes those who do not have the military, economic or political power to make themselves heard (and rewards those who shout the loudest). Wild however at the same time also defined "fostering local ownership" as "enabling local actors to define and lead a process or an initiative or to be in a position of influence in the context of the peacebuilding efforts which are undertaken in their societal environment". This can be interpreted as a willingness to empower those constructive forces that would otherwise be sidelined. The inclusiveness that this stance entails is not only desirable but also bold and courageous—and perhaps for these reasons rather unique in the field. Deeply rooted in Switzerland's tradition of both neutrality in international affairs and inclusive governance at home, it is also reflected in the UN Secretary General's 2012 report on *Strengthening the Role of*

Mediation in the Peaceful Settlement of Disputes, Conflict Prevention and Resolution. The report lists both inclusivity and national ownership as key principles of effective mediation processes and also shows how the two are interlinked (United Nations General Assembly 2012).

Hayman's organization, Peace Direct, aims at strengthening the positive forces within a particular society to increase the chances of success of peacebuilding interventions more generally, not just of mediation processes. She thus put the emphasis on a slightly different concept: "ownership is great, but what we really need is leadership". The idea here is not to arduously squeeze out a compromise between opposed actors that are at best carefully and slowly tiptoeing toward each other, but to instead put all available energy behind selected people who appear to be forging ahead in the 'right' (n.b. as defined by the outsiders) direction. When searching for these positive forces, Peace Direct looks for "entrepreneurs, people who have made sacrifices, who are not in it for the money or personal prestige, and who are good at communicating". The advantage of this approach is that the chosen local actors are certain to own the projects (even though one could also argue the latter are usually very quick in adapting *their* discourse to the requirements of the outsiders). However, whether or not the society as a whole feels ownership is far from being clear, and it is important to keep in mind that "the choice of local partners reflects the principles, values and interests of the outside party" and that it aims at "creating a certain power-shift in the conflict setting" (Reich 2006: 13).

The panellists all agreed that identifying the most relevant actors requires time and effort, but their assessment of the extent of this effort nevertheless differed widely. It appeared as if Wild considered the permanent deployment of twenty 'agents' (globally) into the crisis zones in which interventions are meant to take place as sufficient to gather the necessary understanding of the context. For Schumann, however, international actors' knowledge of civil wars and their consequences on individuals as well as societies remains insufficient as of today, despite the considerable efforts deployed by both practitioners and academics. This insufficiency often does not just mean that the wrong actors are identified, but that the entire programming is based on incorrect assumptions. A pre-condition for fostering local ownership would be the understanding of (various) local perspectives—so far, however, external actors are not interested enough in, for example, "how locals experienced the war" or "what it means to be traumatized". A similar argument was recently put forward by Hellmüller, whose field research in the Democratic Republic of Congo led her to conclude that "the ignorance of local perspectives on questions of authority, conflict sources, and resolution mechanisms led to priority setting by international actors and national elites that was not always in line with local realities" (Hellmüller 2012: 248).

3.3 Structural Challenges

Even if the challenges related to identifying the 'local' were resolved, international actors would still find it rather difficult (i.e. uncomfortable) to transfer real ownership of peacebuilding interventions to these local actors, as the consequences would be far-reaching:

> Taken seriously as a guiding principle for action, local ownership would mean far more than a consulting or participatory role given to the local actors on behalf of the donors or external parties. Rather it means that local actors have the final decisive power over a project's process and outcome. Local ownership then means a power shift, which goes far beyond existing practices. Local actors would not only be involved in the information gathering process or strategy development, but should have the means to decide about the agenda, strategy and budget management themselves, even decide who the beneficiaries of the project should be (Reich 2006: 15).

There are legitimate arguments against local ownership,[4] as stated in an Interpeace chapter: "local actors simply may not have the governance capacities to assume full 'local ownership'" and "a too hands-off approach risks that the various peace and recovery efforts get captured by specific individuals or interest-groups, for their own political benefit and/or for private gain (corruption). 'Local ownership' then reinforces the divisions and antagonisms" (Van Brabant 2010: 2).

In that sense, the 'agenda' of external actors, i.e. the set of values and interests that they represent and which they want to see implemented in practice, is not problematic *per se*. All international actors have such an agenda—otherwise they would not be intervening—and they are thus wary of relinquishing control. Ambassador Wild implicitly illustrated this by saying that "some of the biggest challenges we face [when striving to foster local ownership] are here at home". His institution at times "faces difficulties in explaining creative projects" (with high levels of local ownership) that taxpayers and their representatives only perceive as "doubtful initiatives" whose results are not certain to conform to Swiss ideals and values. What if Swiss taxpayers do not want their government to shake the hands of individuals indicted by the International Criminal Court (a formidable, though not insurmountable, obstacle to the latter's ownership)? Or, on a different level: what if a former warlord isn't ready to 'own' a project that is as gender-sensitive as Swiss taxpayers want 'their' programmes to be?

Taxpayers are not the only obstacles to local ownership which were identified. Reflecting on his experience in UN peacekeeping operations, Schumann drew attention to another challenge as being the lack of interest in ownership by the permanent members of the UN Security Council. He said that the five permanent members, who exert most influence on these missions, are primarily interested in serving their own interests, not those of the host countries or populations. According to him, "from the policy-making level right down to the professional in the peacekeeping operation itself, we find massive resistance to hand over

[4] Also see MacGinty, who warns against the "romanticization of the local" (MacGinty 2011: 51).

responsibility to those we claim to serve". He provided two examples to illustrate this: in Kosovo, the UN mission refused for years to enter into a serious discussion around the former Yugoslav region's status, even though this was by far the local population's most important issue. Similarly, the UN Security Council only intervened in the situation between Sudan and South Sudan when the latter decided to stop its oil production. According to Schumann, the permanent members' interest in the continued flow of oil trumped their interest in peace: as the oil primarily financed the military investments of both neighbours, a production halt could have actually reduced the likelihood of a full-scale war.

Other observers have gone even further. Ole Jacob Sending places the main reason for the fact that local ownership is preached but not practiced in the 'blindness' and 'arrogance' of the peacebuilders. These are, according to him, grounded in two key assumptions:

> The first is that knowledge about universal features and mechanisms of the liberal peacebuilding is more important than geographically specific knowledge of the post-conflict country in question. The second assumption is that the international legitimacy of peacebuilding efforts automatically translates into domestic legitimacy of peacebuilding efforts in post-conflict countries (Sending 2009).

These assumptions represent serious obstacles to local ownership and a significant amount of effort would have to be exerted by the leadership of international peacebuilding institutions in order to address them.

3.4 From Ownership to Inclusiveness…

Having said that, the problems associated with the concept of local ownership would not be resolved even if these unhelpful assumptions were rectified. The real obstacle to its implementation lies in the asymmetrical power relationships between local actors and third party interveners (on that imbalance, see Donais 2009: 15). This is an issue that the panellists could have addressed more explicitly. Granted, scholarly opinion diverges in this regard also depending on how leverage is defined: While Reich has argued that "given the current structures of international cooperation, [local ownership] cannot be seriously implemented" (Reich 2006: 3), Hellmüller recently presented a more nuanced perspective by stating that local actors "also dispose of leverage by the very fact that peacebuilding programmes cannot succeed in the long term without their support and commitment" (Hellmüller 2012: 249). One could also argue that the outsider 'blindness' mentioned above also manifests itself in an inability to perceive the sophisticated strategies of local actors to influence the practical outcomes of projects to their own advantage. However, this then turns into a different discussion, since one would have to say that this local ownership actually refers to a *different* project from the one intended by the international actors. We thus remain with Van Brabant's sober assessment that "there is an intrinsic power-relationship between the one who holds the purse strings and the one who wants to receive the money, and certainly internal actors are not in doubt who really calls the shots" (Van Brabant 2010: 8).

If local ownership cannot be implemented under the current circumstances, wouldn't it be better to 'shoot Bambi', i.e. to abandon the concept altogether, as the keynote speaker of the conference put it? The panellists discussed the option of replacing it with the concept of inclusiveness. The latter is particularly attractive because it can be seen as a means to achieve the former, and the 'bambi' would be able to survive, even if it was removed from the centre of attention. In Wild's words, "local ownership is included in the concept of inclusiveness, whereas in local ownership, inclusiveness isn't necessarily there".

Wild suggested that international actors should support the creation of platforms for dialogue, and that local mediators should be empowered to effectively facilitate these. In this regard, he meets Hayman and the work of Peace Direct, who do just that. Schumann, however, remained sceptical: "If you look at why inclusiveness is in the process of replacing ownership, it's very worrying". There is indeed a danger that once again, a concept is used in donor discourse to justify and embellish their own interventions while covering up the messiness of putting the lofty words into practice. In the end, the same difficult questions of who is to be engaged with, who should get a seat on the 'dialogue platforms', or even who should be capacitated to fill these seats, are answered, again, by the external interveners.

3.5 ...or to Honesty?

One could argue that despite all the challenges identified in this chapter when seeking to implement local ownership, the concept needs to remain 'out there' or 'on the horizon' as a constant reminder to external interveners that they have to *do their best* to (1) gain as much knowledge as possible about the context, including the diversity of local perspectives and the most legitimate actors to represent these and (2) hand over as much as possible of the decision-making power to these actors. Who these actors are is indeed best determined through a process of inclusive dialogue, and here again *doing their best* to identify who should participate in this dialogue is the most that can and should be expected of external actors.

One could also argue, however, that the enormous discrepancy between discourse and practice around this concept actually does more harm than good. Given that it cannot possibly be achieved in the presence of the stark power-imbalances that by definition prevail in settings where peacebuilding interventions are taking place, and given the huge transaction costs that would be associated with serious implementation, the 'false talk' should be abandoned. Rather than claiming to foster local ownership, external actors should instead commit to openness around the challenges faced, and to 'honest dialogue'.

Honest dialogue would imply that external actors transparently communicate their values and visions to the societies in which they plan to intervene.[5] It would need to be accompanied by an honest declaration as regards the negotiability of the external actor's objectives and approaches (i.e. the extent of the willingness of this actor to allow for local influence—or 'ownership'), and by a dialogue to negotiate these. Reich has suggested the concept of "learning sites" (Reich 2006: 23), i.e. spaces allocated to mutual learning between outsiders and insiders throughout a particular intervention. The commitment to honesty would already start ahead of the intervention, however, and would clarify and delimit areas of information, consultation and negotiation. A similar differentiation is made by Van Brabant, who distinguishes between "public acceptance without participation", "public participation", and "public consultations" (Van Brabant 2010: 4). The transparent communication of these parameters would not only be more respectful toward local actors, but would also represent the first step on the path to a more equal relationship.

References

Autesserre, Séverine, 2010: *The Trouble with the Congo: Local Violence and the Failure of International Peacebuilding* (New York: Cambridge University Press).

Brabant, Koenraad van, 2010: "Peacebuilding How? Broad Local Ownership" (Geneva: Interpeace); at: http://www.interpeace.org/publications/doc_download/143-peacebuilding-how-broad-local-ownership-english (1 April 2013).

Chade, Jamil, 2012: "The Conflict and Fragility Agenda Post-Busan: Directions, Opportunities, Challenges" (Geneva: Geneva Peacebuilding Platform); at: http://www.genevadeclarationorg/fileadmin/docs/general/GD-GPB-Brief2-Conflict-fragility-post-Busan.pdf (1 April 2013).

Donais, Timothy, 2009: "Empowerment or Imposition? Dilemmas of Local Ownership in Post-Conflict Peacebuilding Processes", in: *Peace & Change* 34, 1: 3–26.

Hellmüller, Sara, 2012: "The Ambiguities of Local Ownership: Evidence from the Democratic Republic of Congo", in: *African Security*, 5, 3–4: 236–254.

MacGinty, Roger, 2011: *International Peacebuilding and Local Resistance: Hybrid Forms of Peace* (New York: Palgrave Macmillan).

Reich, Hannah, 2006: *"Local Ownership" in Conflict Transformation Projects*, Berghof Occasional Paper (Berlin: Berghof Research Center for Constructive Conflict Management).

Sending, Ole Jacob, 2009: *Why Peacebuilders Fail to Secure Ownership and Be Sensitive to Context*, NUPI Working Paper, Security in Practice (Oslo: Norwegian Institute of International Affairs).

United Nations General Assembly, 2012: *Strengthening the Role of Mediation in the Peaceful Settlement of Disputes, Conflict Prevention and Resolution—Report of the Secretary General* (New York: United Nations).

[5] A transparent communication on the external actor's interests would of course also be desirable, but appears too unrealistic as to justify being included here.

Part II
Case Studies

Customary chief observes reconciliation ceremony in Berunda, DR Congo. *Source* Sara Hellmüller/swisspeace. The permission to reproduce this photo was granted.

Chapter 4
Traditional Authorities, Local Justice and Local Conflict Resolution Mechanisms in South Sudan

Martina Santschi

Abstract This chapter explores local justice and conflict resolution mechanisms using the example of South Sudan. By describing and critically discussing different arenas of local justice and conflict resolution mechanisms, it contributes to reflections on the meaning of the term 'local' in South Sudan. The chapter illustrates that chiefs play a significant role in local justice as well as in conflict resolution in South Sudan. In addition, the chapter exemplifies that 'local level', 'grassroots' conflict resolution mechanisms are multi-layered and frequently involve regional and national government institutions as well as external actors such as UN agencies, international donors and international NGOs that support peace initiatives and peace conferences.

Keywords Traditional authorities · Local justice · Chiefs · South Sudan · 'Local' · Conflict resolution mechanisms · Peace conference · Wunlit · Dinka · 'People-to-people peace process'

4.1 Introduction

The first panel of the swisspeace annual peace conference 2012 discussed 'peacebuilding from a local perspective'. Del Rumdit Deng, Director of Traditional Authorities of the Local Government Board of the Government of South Sudan, spoke about the role of traditional authorities in local justice and conflict

I would like to thank Sara Hellmüller, Michaela Ledesma and Naomi Pendel for the review of the text.

M. Santschi (✉)
swisspeace, Bern, Switzerland
University of Bern, Bern, Switzerland
e-mail: martina.santschi@swisspeace.ch

S. Hellmüller and M. Santschi (eds.), *Is Local Beautiful?*,
SpringerBriefs in Environment, Security, Development and Peace 11,
DOI: 10.1007/978-3-319-00306-1_4,

resolution in South Sudan. The following paragraphs attempt to explore what kind of local justice and conflict resolution mechanisms exist in South Sudan. By describing and critically discussing different arenas of local justice and conflict resolution mechanisms, this chapter aims at contributing to reflections on the meaning of the term 'local'. This chapter is based on Del Rumdit's presentation, on recent publications on the topic, as well as on research conducted in South Sudan, in particular in Northern Bahr el-Ghazal State.

4.2 Chiefs and Chiefly Institutions in South Sudan

Chiefs and other forms of traditional authorities play a pivotal role in local justice arenas and in conflict resolution mechanisms. Before exploring their engagement in these fields, chiefs and chiefly institutions are briefly introduced.[1]

4.2.1 The Invention of Tradition: History of Chiefs and Chief Courts

Administrative chieftaincies were introduced in relation to the establishment of the native administration by the Anglo-Egyptian Condominium government. Similarly, present-day chief courts date back to the Condominium era (Johnson 1986). Yet, engagements of chiefs in chief courts as well as in local conflict resolution mechanisms relate to pre-colonial practices and institutions. Before the introduction of administrative chiefs (*bany alath* in Dinka)[2] and chief courts during the colonial era, spiritual leaders such as Dinka spear masters (*bany biith*) solved intra-communal disputes and mediated in inter-clan conflicts (Mawson 1989).

4.2.2 Chief Relations to the Government: In Between the Government and the Community

Chiefs are strongly related to local government institutions in view of chieftaincies' colonial roots. Subsequent governments have shaped their structures as well as their area of work (Höhne 2008). In addition, their role and chiefly structures are at least partially defined by current legislation. Chiefs own according to the Local

[1] In this chapter individuals who occupy administrative chieftaincies are referred to as chiefs. However, all other forms of leaders who date back to the pre-colonial era, such as elders, spiritual leaders, cattle camp leaders and clan heads, are referred to as traditional authorities.

[2] The tern *bany alath* is widely used in Dinka communities in Northern Bahr el-Ghazal State.

Government Act a "semi-autonomous" (GoSS 2009: 11) status and are mandated to engage in a number of activities including the provision of "customary law and justice in the customary law courts" (*Ibid*). The Local Government Act (2009) furthermore refers to differing levels of chiefs such as paramount chiefs, head chiefs, executive chiefs, sub-chiefs and headmen. Yet, chiefs are at the same time (s)elected as well as potentially dismissed by community members. Thus, they are accountable to their communities. Furthermore, they relate to pre-colonial socio-political and spiritual institutions, practices and norms (Santschi 2014). Accordingly, chiefs are associated both with the sphere of the state as well as the sphere of the society. South Sudanese interviewees recurrently connect chiefs with local government as well as with the community.

Present Day Chieftaincies

Chiefly institutions in South Sudan differ from area to area. In Aweil East County, in Northern Bahr el-Ghazal for instance, three levels of administrative chiefs existed up to 2011; the executive chiefs (*alama thith*), the sub-chiefs (*alama chol*) and the gol leaders (*nhom gol*). In 2011, partly in line with the Local Government Act (2009), a new level of chiefs—the paramount chiefs—was introduced in Northern Bahr el-Ghazal State.[3]

Whereas executive and sub-chiefs relate to the 'traditional' socio-political entities called cattle camps (*wuot*) in Northern Bahr el-Ghazal State, gol leaders head hereditary entities, mostly lineages. As a consequence, executive and sub-chiefs lead groups of people who are not related to each other through kinship ties, while gol leaders are usually responsible for a group of people who are their paternal relatives (Santschi 2014).

The succession of chiefs follows dissimilar rules in different areas in South Sudan. In some areas chiefs are elected while in others chiefs are selected from chiefly families. Chieftaincies in Aweil East County and other areas in Northern Bahr el-Ghazal State for instance are mostly 'inherited' within chiefly lineages. However, in other areas—for example in Jonglei in areas inhabited by Lou Nuer—chieftaincies are seemingly open to all families (Interview with a chief, Jonglei, February 2013). Shilluk and Anyuak feature kingships that are passed on in royal families.

In Dinka and Nuer communities the capability of chiefs to serve the interests of their communities is considered pivotal. Furthermore, chiefs are expected to conform to social norms by being truthful, unbiased and supportive of community members in addition to actively promoting peace and harmony (Lienhardt 2003). Accordingly, chiefs are anticipated to act as role models. Chiefs who do not fulfil the expectations of their communities and who transgress social norms, for instance by accepting bribes, might be dismissed (Mawson 1989). In the case of Jonglei, where chiefs were elected in 2012, some chiefs who lost the support of

[3] In practice a number of the existing executive chiefs were promoted to paramount chiefs.

their communities were not re-elected (Interview with a chief, Jonglei, February 2013). Accordingly, chiefs can be held accountable by community members.

Chiefs engage in a number of different activities at the local level in South Sudan. They settle disputes in chief courts, they engage in peace processes, collect taxes, allocate food aid, act as intermediaries between the government and the community and they mobilize community members for projects. This chapter focuses on chief engagement in local justice and conflict resolution.

4.3 Local Justice: Informal Justice Arenas and Chief Courts

Chiefs and other forms of traditional authorities engage in different arenas of local justice and play an active role in various conflict resolution mechanisms in South Sudan. These arenas of justice range from informal gatherings to formal hearings in chief courts.

Elders, family and clan heads, cattle camp leaders, spiritual leaders and chiefs in many cases settle disputes in informal arenas of justice at the family and village level. Only conflicts that were not solved informally are opened in formal chief courts or in county courts, which constitute statuary courts (Leonardi et al. 2010). Chief courts, in which cases are settled according to customary law, are of great importance as major provider of justice in South Sudan (Deng 2011; Höhne 2008; Leonardi et al. 2010). Van Cutsem and Galand suggested that "around 90 % of disputes are settled before the customary courts" (2007: 11).

4.3.1 Chief Court Structures and Chief Court Practices

Chief court structures and chief court practices are at variance from area to area in South Sudan (Leonardi et al. 2010). In Aweil East County, Northern Bahr el-Ghazal State for instance up to 2010 each payam featured a payam court, a regional chief court and several executive chief courts (Santschi 2014). Chiefs and chief courts are according to the Local Government Act (2009) subject to local government institutions thus they report to payam administrators and to the county executive. The county and the payam executive are furthermore thought to be supervising chief courts (Leonardi et al. 2010).

Furthermore, the Local Government Act (2009) does not determine the role and activities of chiefs in detail, but leaves these decisions open to local level decision making institutions: the county legislative assemblies. However, in a number of the counties county legislative assemblies do not yet exist. As a consequence, the functions of chiefs are not determined in contemporary legislations. In addition, the Local Government Act (2009) has not yet been fully implemented. Accordingly, in practice, chiefs' activities relate to former, long established areas of work and are at the same time constantly negotiated between chiefs, community members, officials of the local government and other key stakeholders in local political arenas (Santschi 2014).

Cases tried in chief courts often involve parties of conflict that live in the same payam or even in the same village. Therefore, chiefs commonly apply more restorative and retributive rather than punitive judicial practices as this approach promotes stability and reconciliation within communities (Jok et al. 2004). Although chief courts are open to the public and community members are free to participate in discussions during trials, in Northern Bahr el-Ghazal State women in most cases only attend trials when they are litigants (Golooba-Mutebi/Mapuor 2005; Santschi 2014). Accordingly, women seemingly do not participate as actively as men in debates in chief courts.

4.3.2 Common Cases Tried in Chief Courts

Disputes settled in chief courts relate to prevalent livelihood systems. In agro-pastoralist and pastoralist communities, conflicts over livestock—in particular cattle—prevail. Conflicts over cattle emerge for instance over access and control of cattle, claims over cattle loans and cattle theft. Furthermore, bride wealth, which is for instance in Dinka and Nuer communities mostly distributed among paternal relatives of the bride, is often a source of dispute between grooms and their in-laws as well as between relatives of the bride (Santschi 2014). Other common court cases relate to adultery, elopement, and divorce in addition to brawling (Leonardi et al. 2010). Impoverished community members moreover in some occurrences open court cases against community members and relatives to enforce support for instance in the form of sorghum, money or livestock.

In addition to that, chiefs and spiritual leaders play a pivotal role in the settling of homicide cases. They do so in spite of the fact that homicide cases, according to South Sudanese legislation, ought to be tried in statuary courts. In Dinka communities for instance, families of a killed person potentially respond to a lethal accident or homicide with revenge. They take revenge either by attempting to kill the perpetrator or his relatives. Chiefs and other traditional authorities frequently prevent such acts of revenge by conducting rituals and by initiating compensation negotiations between the conflict parties (Santschi 2014). In connection to such negotiations the families of the victims commonly open court cases against the perpetrators instead of taking the law into their own hands. By preventing acts of revenge, chiefs and spiritual leaders impede the eruption of intra- and inter-communal violence (Kocjok/dut Majak 1990).[4]

[4] Moreover, chiefs commonly have the responsibility to collect compensation cattle. In Dinka communities in Northern Bahr el-Ghazal State, the compensation for a human death is 31 heads of cattle that are collected by the chiefs among clan members close to the perpetrator.

Furthermore, specific types of land conflicts are settled in chief courts. In agro-pastoralist and agricultural communities conflicts over arable land and fields at times emerge between neighbours. Such conflicts are, for instance in Northern Bahr el-Ghazal State, usually settled by headmen and sub-chiefs (Santschi 2014). Conflicts over land also develop between returnees and hosts. During the past armed conflicts, numerous South Sudanese were displaced within Sudan as well as in neighbouring countries. Since the signing of the *Comprehensive Peace Agreement* (CPA) in 2005, countless displaced South Sudanese have returned to South Sudan. In the Equatorial region as well as other regions of South Sudan disputes over land ownership emerged between returnees and South Sudanese, who during the civil war settled in homes and on the land of then-*internally displaced persons* (IDPs) and refugees.

Differing Perceptions of Chief Courts and Chief Courts Practices

Interviewees from Northern Bahr el-Ghazal and other areas underlined that they have a positive view of chief court practices in general (Leonardi et al. 2010; Golooba-Mutebi/Mapuor 2005; Santschi 2014). Chief court practices were by interviewees of Leonardi et al. often depicted as "fair and nondiscriminatory" (2010: 39). Other positive characteristics associated with chief courts were the chiefs' acknowledgment of the context and the background of disputes, their retributive practices in addition to speedy procedures (Harragin 2007; Leonardi et al. 2010; Mennen 2008).

Leonardi et al. however, as well stated to "obstacles to justice and personal security [that] are still seen to be the extensive militarization of young men, police incompetence or abuses, the power and corruption of the government, and the perceived relative erosion of the power of elders, chiefs, and even judges" (2010: 39). In addition some chief court members are accused of corruptive practices and biases (Santschi 2014). However, interviewees primarily criticized statuary law courts for being corrupt, distant, and hard 'to comprehend' (Leonardi et al. 2010; Van Cutsem/Galand 2007).

Despite the by and large positive reputation of chief courts by South Sudanese interviewees, chief court practices are criticized by South Sudanese and expatriates. The critique points at practices that do not comply with international human right standards in addition to discriminatory practices against women, youth and minority groups (Santschi 2014). Women are considered discriminated against in reference to divorces, gender based violence and ownership of land and property (Jok et al. 2004; Santschi 2014). One example of customary law practice that is widely panned by actors advocating human rights is the marriage of rape victims with rapists. From an emic thus local perspective, this practice aims at protecting the social status as well as the "marital rights" (Leonardi et al. 2010: 61) of the victim and her family.

Scholars such as Deng (2011) and Jok et al. (2004) refer to the importance of the reform of chief court practices in particular in relation to women's rights. Yet, they also suggest that reform processes should be driven by South Sudanese: "There is consensus amongst those interviewed, that change to customary law is inevitable but change must come from within Sudanese society and at a pace, to which society can adjust" (Jok et al. 2004: 6).

In view of their engagement in local justice, chiefs and other forms of traditional authorities prevent disputes from escalating into armed conflicts between different families, clans and communities. Accordingly, chiefs foster stability and "maintain public order" (Harragin 2007: 14) both within and between communities. However, chiefs and chief court influence is limited and disputes are not necessarily brought to court but may be solved by vigilantism. Whereas in some areas of South Sudan such as Northern Bahr el-Ghazal State armed intra-communal conflicts are no longer prevalent, in other areas they continue to exist.

4.3.3 'Local' Conflict Resolution Mechanisms: Special Courts, Inter-Communal Meetings and Peace Processes

While chief courts and informal arenas of justice settle mostly intra-communal disputes, inter-communal conflicts are often addressed in other forums conflict resolution such as special courts, inter-communal meetings and in peace processes.

The structures, practices as well as the composition of stakeholders of these differing forums and mechanisms vary. Whereas some meetings only include chiefs, other forums bring together different stakeholders such as chiefs, church leaders, women leaders, youth representatives, politicians as well as representatives of *community based organizations* (CBOs) and international agencies. While special courts are formalized institutions, other forums and processes are more informal and temporary. Furthermore, some of these mechanisms are supported by international agencies, *non-governmental organizations* (NGOs) and bilateral partners whereas others are not. Yet, in practice, the line between these differing forums and mechanisms is often blurred.

Causes for Inter-Communal Conflicts

Inter-communal disputes are caused by different points of contention in present-day South Sudan. Access to pasture and water for livestock is an important source of conflict involving agro-pastoralist and pastoralist communities. In particular, conflicts are prevalent during the dry season when numerous pastoralists and agro-pastoralists move their livestock to swampy lowland areas (*toic*) in search of water and grazing land (Santschi 2014). Furthermore, some agro-pastoralists—for instance Lou Nuer communities in Uror County in Jonglei state—have to enter pasture of other communities in neighbouring counties to access grazing during dry season (Interview with a government official, Jonglei, February 2013).[5]

[5] Livestock movements regularly cause disputes between herders on the one side and agro-pastoralists and agriculturalists on the other side when livestock destroys fields and gardens.

While disputes over arable land frequently engage members of the same community, conflicts over pasture and water sources often emerge between different communities and potentially differing ethnic groups.[6] The settlement of conflicts over pasture and water access often involves senior chiefs in addition to higher government officials, administrators and other stakeholders. Accordingly, these conflicts are addressed at a higher administrative and political level than disputes over arable land.

A further source of inter-communal conflicts in South Sudan is cattle raiding. Cattle raiding occurs between various agro-pastoralist and pastoralist groups including different Dinka, Nuer, Murle and Toposa. Raided cattle are a source of wealth (in particular bride wealth), status and fame. Herders and other community members are regularly killed in the course of cattle raids. Cattle raids and homicide related to cattle raids often lead to revenge attacks and foster inter-communal violence.

Although cattle raiding is not a new phenomenon in South Sudan, its dynamics have changed. As a result of past civil wars and militarization of South Sudanese communities cattle raiding nowadays involves modern weapons and it is often related to past grievances and inter-communal tensions rooted in previous hostilities.[7] In recent years, cattle raiding and inter-communal violence linked to cattle raids have claimed the lives of many South Sudanese. One of the infamous, more recent, examples of cattle raids and inter-communal violence occurred in Jonglei between Murle, Dinka and Nuer communities (Small Arms Survey 2012).

Moreover, power struggles and political tensions are supposedly further causes for inter-communal violence. Disputes over marital rights, elopement, cattle theft and murder may also unleash inter-communal armed conflicts. While cattle raiding and inter-communal fighting are prevalent in certain areas such as Jonglei, Warrap and Lakes State, in other areas—for instance in Northern Bahr-el Ghazal State—it is no longer common.[8]

Special Courts, Inter-communal Meetings, Peace Processes and Peace Conferences

Cattle raiding, inter-communal violence related to cattle raiding and inter-communal violence in general are not commonly settled in chief courts but in other conflict resolution forums such as special courts, inter-communal meetings and through peace processes.

---

[6] While arable land is mostly 'used' by households, pasture is generally used and controlled by communities (Mawson 1989).

[7] Since the past civil war, established rules in warfare, such as the sparing of women, children and elders from violent attacks, are frequently ignored (Agwanda/Harris 2009; Beswick 1998; Bradbury et al. 2006).

[8] Respondents from Northern Bahr el-Ghazal State argued that in view of the devastating *Murahaleen* raids of the past civil war, Dinka from today's Northern Bahr el-Ghazal halted intra and inter-communal fighting within the state (Santschi 2014).

In October 2010, two 'special courts' were for instance established in Warrap State to counter insecurity, inter-communal violence and cattle raiding. The state governor mandated two men including a paramount chief to solve homicide cases related to past cattle raids, other crimes and revenge attacks between different communities in the special court.[9] Accordingly, special courts are established to settle disputes and armed conflict that occur between members of different communities and partly also by members of different ethnic groups.

Furthermore, chiefs are involved in mechanisms that aim at preventing and settling conflicts between differing groups in inter-communal meetings, peace processes and peace conferences. Senior chiefs together with officials, educated members of the political elite, church representatives, and spiritual leaders, youth and women leaders in addition to other stakeholders regularly engage in peace processes, dialogues and peace conferences involving neighbouring groups that are in conflict.

4.3.4 History of Resolution of Intra-Communal Conflicts and Traditional Authorities

The role of traditional leaders as mediators dates back to the pre-colonial era. Before the arrival of the Turko-Egyptian powers, spiritual leaders—in the case of the Dinka, the spear masters (*bany biith*)—engaged in mediation and conducted rituals that aimed at preventing further armed encounters between parties of conflict. Engagement in peacemaking and mediation has been in the past and is up to the present time associated with fame and political influence (Lienhardt 2003; Santschi 2014).

Inter-communal meetings organized by government institutions also have a long history in South Sudan. In an attempt to prevent or to settle conflicts over access to pasture and water, the Anglo-Egyptian Condominium government introduced regular meetings between different communities who had yearly encounters during the dry season in view of livestock migration. Representatives of the respective communities met before the livestock migration to discuss access to pasture and water sources thus migration routes and the timeframe of the migration. In addition to that, before the migrating herders left, disputes for instance over cattle theft and elopement were solved in conjoint chief courts (Bradbury et al. 2006).[10]

---

[9] Gurtong; at: http://www.gurtong.net/ECM/Editorial/tabid/124/ctl/ArticleView/mid/519/articleId/4293/Insecurity-Special-Court-Established-in-Warrap-State.aspx (3 March 2013).

[10] In relation to livestock migration, conflicts between farmers and herders regularly emerge when livestock destroys fields.

4.3.5 *Peace Conferences and Peace Processes: Two Examples*

Inter-communal meetings aiming at negotiating access to pasture and to discuss and settle ongoing conflicts in different parts of South Sudan have taken place since the 1990s. The following paragraphs explore two examples of peace processes and meetings. Thereby the complex nature of such processes, the involvement of local, regional, national and international actors as well as strengths and challenges are touched upon.

The Wunlit Peace Conference

The first example refers to the Wunlit peace conference of 1999.[11] The Wunlit peace conference took place during the past civil war (1983–2005) and aimed at settling inter-communal hostilities between Southern Sudanese groups. The conference in Wunlit of 1999 is widely known and constituted a benchmark for subsequent peace processes and peace conferences in Southern Sudan. "Wunlit was, it seems now, unique. Its extensive documentation and enduring achievement mean that it has become a marker against which other local peacemaking processes in Sudan are measured" (Bradbury et al. 2006: 28).

The Wunlit conference was organized and facilitated by the New Sudan Council of Churches (NSCC) (Beyna et al. 2001).[12] Before preparing the Wunlit peace conference, beginning in 1997, NSCC engaged in a dialogue with the Sudan People's Liberation Movement/Sudan People's Liberation Army (SPLM/A).[13] Finally the NSCC and the SPLM/A agreed to collaborate in peacemaking and reconciliation (Agwanda/Harris 2009).[14] Despite the backing of the SPLM/A,

[11] Riek Machar and his troops as well engaged in local peace processes. One example was a peace process between Jikany and Lou Nuer in Akobo in 1994 (Jenner 2000).

[12] The NSCC emerged in the 1980s as an ecumenical organization working in SPLA controlled areas (Bradbury et al. 2006; Jenner 2000). The Sudan Council of Churches was active in GoS controlled areas.

[13] NSCC and the SPLM/A had a difficult relation as the NSCC tried to keep distance to all parties in conflict (Bradbury et al. 2006). In the early 1990s numerous attempts to foster reconciliation failed.

[14] The SPLM/A had an ambiguous relation to the Wunlit peace conference. While John Garang, the Commander in Chief of the SPLA and the Chairman of the SPLM, was only to a limited degree sympathetic, Salva Kiir, his Deputy, was supportive of the peace process (Bradbury et al. 2006). The side of Riek Machar backed the conference after being convinced by the NSCC. President Bashir expressed the willingness to back the process but later the Government of Sudan (GoS) armed Paulino Matiep, a Bul Nuer militia leader, who refused to join the conference (Beyna et al. 2001; Bradbury et al. 2006).

the NSCC followed a people-to-people peacemaking approach focusing on community groups in conflict and not on political and military groups (Bradbury et al. 2006).

The people-to-people peacemaking approach of the NSCC aimed at "a deliberate and facilitated process that encourages communities, leaders and people involved in conflict situations to reach agreements among themselves for stopping conflicts, achieving reconciliation and promoting healing, peace and justice among and for people in their communities" (NSCC 2002: 2 cited in Agwanda and Harris 2009: 43). Thus the Wunlit conference focused on intra and inter-communal hostilities in Southern Sudan and not on the war between the *Government of Sudan* (GoS) and SPLM/A. People-to-people peace processes "distinguished from state-level diplomacy is the far greater level of public participation and, in most cases, the absence of international and government mediation" (Bradbury et al. 2006: 16). Parallel to the people-to-people process, negotiations went on at the national level between GoS and SPLM/A. This peace process that started in 1994 was facilitated by *Inter-Governmental Authority on Development* (IGAD) (Bradbury et al. 2006; Jenner 2000).[15]

From February 27 to March 8, 1999 representatives of Dinka and Nuer living on the West Bank of the Nile met for a peace and reconciliation conference in Wunlit in today's Tonj East County, Warrap State.[16] The Wunlit conference aimed at settling armed conflicts and fostering dialogue and reconciliation between Dinka and Nuer communities. In the 1990s members of these communities engaged in inter-communal armed conflicts that were promoted by the split of the SPLM/A in 1991 and by militarization.[17] Established mechanisms to prevent large scale hostilities and mutual relations between the communities were negatively affected by the civil war and militarization (Bradbury et al. 2006).

The Wunlit peace conference featured the broad participation of elders, youth, women, chiefs, spiritual leaders, intellectuals, and members of the diaspora of the respective communities. In addition officials, administrators, representatives of the SPLM/A and Nuer militias and representatives of neighbouring groups participated as observers (Beyna et al. 2001). Accordingly, the Wunlit peace conference was a dialogue "between civilians, rather than politicians" (Bradbury et al. 2006: 42).

The Wunlit conference focused on dialogue, negotiations, reconciliation and forgiveness. During the conference participants sat together, discussed grievances, causes of conflicts and narrated stories. In addition to that, rituals such as the sacrificing of white bulls were conducted (Bradbury et al. 2006). Accordingly, 'traditional' institutions and practices of conflict resolution were considered in Wunlit. The participants agreed on a number of points that were reflected in a

---

[15] IGAD member states were Sudan, Eritrea, Ethiopia, Djibouti, Somalia, Kenya, and Uganda (Jenner 2000).

[16] Ahead of the Wunlit conference, workshops and reciprocal meetings to foster trust building in the respective communities were held (Bradbury et al. 2006).

[17] In 1991, the Riek Machar together with Lam Akol and Gordon Kong declared that they had overthrown John Garang. They founded the SPLM/A Nasir (Bradbury et al. 2006).

covenant. The agreement encompassed among other points the cessation of hostile acts, freedom of movement, sharing of pasture and water, the return of abductees in addition to the establishment of border courts and a Dinka-Nuer Peace Council (Beyna et al. 2001; Local Government Board 2011).

After the conference, armed clashes between the involved communities stopped, raiding and abduction were temporarily halted and abductees were returned. In addition to that the respective groups started to share pasture and water and trade resumed (Beyna et al. 2001; Bradbury et al. 2006; Jenner 2000). Moreover, due to the improved security, aid was more easily delivered (Beyna et al. 2001). In contrast to other subsequent conferences, Wunlit was and still is considered as successful (Bradbury et al. 2006). After the conference, the Dinka Nuer peace council started to meet to ensure the continued abidance to the recommendations (Bradbury et al. 2006). They met for instance in 2001 in view of the threat of inter-communal conflicts.

Since the conference in Wunlit, hundreds of other 'grassroots' peace meetings and examples of inter-communal dialogue have been conducted in present-day South Sudan with the facilitation of the NSCC, other church institutions and Christian NGOs such as IKV Pax Christi (Beyna et al. 2001; Bradbury et al. 2006). Furthermore, international actors including Pact, Christian Aid, Oxfam, the *United States Agency for International Development* (USAID) *United Nations Development Programme* (UNDP) and *United Nations Children's Fund* (UNICEF) funded such processes and started to engage in local level peacemaking themselves by adapting people-to-people peace processes (Bradbury et al. 2006). "What arguably began as an indigenous (if externally brokered) process managed by the churches, the SPLM/A and Southern civil activists, has become part of a broader political and developmental strategy by external agents" (Bradbury et al. 2006: 27).[18]

The Wunlit conference, similar to other 'grassroots' peace conferences and processes, was however also criticized. Despite the fact that it achieved the settlement of conflicts between the involved neighbouring communities, the Wunlit peace conference did not tackle the armed conflict between the GoS and the SPLM/A and its causes (Beyna et al. 2001). Consequently, "structural factors underlying the war" (Bradbury et al. 2006: 8) including diverging economic development, different political representation, unequal access to services and perceived disparate political rights were not addressed.

A further point of criticism is the temporality of peace conferences and peacemaking (Beyna et al. 2001). Peace conferences are temporary events and the recommendations are not binding. Criticism pointed at the inadequate implementation of recommendations and agreements, lack of follow-up and peacebuilding activities by NSCC and other institutions that facilitated such conferences (Agwanda/Harris 2009; Bradbury et al. 2006; Jenner 2000). In an evaluation in 2000, reviewers recommended the NSCC consider "institutionalising local peace

[18] Bradbury et al. (2006) questioned however whether any of the international actors could have arranged an event that was as effective as the Wunlit peace conference.

agreements through the creation of peace councils and ecumenical centres, supporting further reconciliation conferences, developing strategic linkages with the military factions and international forums and building the NSCC's own institutional capacity" (Bradbury et al. 2006: 45).

Follow-up and long-term peacebuilding activities are thought to be needed to foster sustainable conflict transformation. Accordingly, further engagement including the delivery of services, rule of law and development should follow peace conferences that tackle underlining causes of conflict (Agwanda/Harris 2009). The NSCC to some degree engaged in service delivery but its main focus was on peacemaking. In practice, peacebuilding in the broad sense including service delivery are often beyond the capacity and competences of local actors such as NSCC. International actors that funded and supported peace conferences, however, were not supporting longer-term peacebuilding efforts including service delivery after the Wunlit conference (Bradbury et al. 2006). Yet, gradually international NGOs and agencies changed their approach and started to engage in peacebuilding including service delivery, infrastructure establishment, development and livelihood support (Bradbury et al. 2006).

The Wunlit peace conference, similar to other peace conferences and processes, was not isolated from national and regional political developments and agendas. National and regional political contestations frequently also manifest themselves at the local level as the example of the SPLM/A split of 1991 demonstrates (Bradbury et al. 2006). The GoS was not supportive of the conference as it aimed at uniting Southern Sudanese (Bradbury et al. 2006). Although the SPLM/A was at the beginning generally supportive, its leadership apparently refused to participate in a subsequent meeting in Kisumu organized by the NSCC to avoid being criticized for following the agenda of unity with the North (Bradbury et al. 2006).

Thus, local peace conferences in what was then Southern Sudan clearly had a political dimension. In view of demands for separation, international actors feared that 'grassroots' processes might hamper peace negotiations with the GoS and were more and more reluctant to support such conferences. The NSCC was furthermore criticized for being too close to the SPLM/A (Bradbury et al. 2006).

The Wunlit peace agreement, despite being described as a success, was apparently only temporarily effective. During the last years, cattle raiding and armed inter-communal violence was prevalent between the respective Dinka and Nuer communities living on the West Bank of the Nile in Unity State, Warrap State and Lakes State. For instance in September 2011 the county commissioner of Mayendit County, in Unity State accused neighbours from Tonj East County, in Warrap State of having attacked his community killing at least 28 individuals.[19]

On several recent occasions, representatives of the respective communities called for an end to the cattle raids. In January 2009, a peace conference was organized in Yirol involving participants from the three states calling among other

[19] Sudan Tribune; at: http://www.sudantribune.com/spip.php?iframe&page=imprimable&id_article=40125 (1 October 2013).

things for the formation of border courts, disarmament of civilians and compensation payment (Local Government Board 2011). A conference document stated that the conference aimed at "reviewing the past resolutions that were passed (Bentiu, Maria-Iou and Yirol conferences) yet none of them was implemented" (Local Government Board 2011). In February 2011, chiefs from Warrap and Lakes State met for two days to discuss the prevention of future cattle raids.[20] In relation to the meeting, a commissioner of the affected counties informed about the establishment of a special court to solve and compensate cattle theft.

In September 2012, commissioners and paramount chiefs from the three states vowed during a peace conference to stop cattle raiding.[21] In April 2013, Members of Parliament from Unity, Warrap and Lakes States "agreed to mobilize their young men to stop the cattle raids that create insecurity across state and county borders, preventing trade and other ties between the neighbouring communities".[22] The parliamentarians asked for a conference and agreed to "revise the 2002 WUNLIT peace talks that were signed by neighbouring chiefs along bordering states for reconsideration in order to eliminate cattle raiding".[23] Thus, political representatives currently call for a revision of Wunlit to halt raids and conflicts.

Although the Wunlit peace conference was represented and is still regarded as the paramount example of a 'grassroots', 'people-to-people' and 'bottom-up' peace conference in what was then Southern Sudan, its nature and background is much more complex and multi-layered. Southern intellectuals initiated the process that led to the conference and NSCC was based in Kenya (Bradbury et al. 2006). The SPLM/A or at least influential members of the SPLM/A supported the reconciliation and peacemaking activities. In addition to that, the Wunlit conference and following meetings were funded and partly facilitated by external donors, international agencies and international NGOs (Beyna et al. 2001). Therefore they were clearly linked to the international sphere. Bradbury et al. 2006 argued.

> However, the people-to-people process was not strictly-speaking a grassroots movement. It was instigated by churches and southern intellectuals and funded by external parties. Furthermore, as the NSCC (NSCC 2002b: 50–53) also recognized, it relied on the military powers in the South for security: "there can be no peace without the full support of the military and militia factions in the area… grassroots peace will not stand if factions continue to fight". The success of Wunlit was dependent on this support from the SPLM/A. The Liliir and other East Bank initiatives were less successful because of its absence (Bradbury et al. 2006: 53).

Consequently, the broad support of the Wunlit peace process including the backing of the SPLM/A led to its success (Bradbury et al. 2006).

---

20 Miraya FM; at: http://reliefweb.int/report/sudan/sudan-warrap-and-lakes-chiefs-push-peaceful-coexistence (4 March 2013).

21 Sudan Tribune; at: http://www.sudantribune.com/spip.php?article43899 (7 July 2013).

22 Sudan Tribune; at: http://www.sudantribune.com/spip.php?article46197 (7 July 2013).

23 Sudan Tribune; at: http://www.sudantribune.com/spip.php?article46197 (7 July 2013).

The Dinka Malwal–Misseriya Peace Conference and Negotiations Over Access to Natural Resources

The second example refers to recent negotiations and a peace conference between Dinka Malwal from Northern Bahr el-Ghazal State, South Sudan and Misseriya from South Kordofan, Sudan. The conference took place in 2008, during the interim period, thus after the signing of the Comprehensive Peace Agreement in 2005 that ended the armed conflict between the GoS and the SPLA.

Dinka Malwal and Misseriya have a long history of conflicts over pasture and water. At the same time, the two communities are linked through trade as well as marriage and kinship ties and share similar livelihood systems. During the Condominium rule, representatives of the two communities conducted annual meetings to settle disputes and to negotiate access to pasture and water. However, the abolishment of chiefs in present-day Sudan in the early 1970s negatively affected the negotiations between the two communities (Bradbury et al. 2006; Mathok 2010).

During the past civil war, relations between Dinka Malwal and Misseriya deteriorated. While a part of the Misseriya youth joined the *Murahaleen* militias that raided what is today Northern Bahr el-Ghazal State, numerous Dinka Malwal fought on the side of the SPLA against *Murahaleen* and the GoS.[24] Nevertheless, local level negotiations without external funding started in the early 1990s with Misseriya traders. These negotiations led to the opening of peace markets in Northern Bahr el-Ghazal State and other states bordering present-day Sudan (Bradbury et al. 2006).[25] The opening of the markets improved the access to goods in what is today Northern Bahr el-Ghazal State. Since the establishment of the peace market, a Dinka Malwal-Misseriya peace committee exists in Warawar that settles conflicts between different traders.

In November 2008, a peace conference between Dinka Malwal and Misseriya took place in Aweil town, the capital of Northern Bahr el-Ghazal State. The conference was organized as a response to clashes that occurred between the SPLA and Misseriya in late 2007 and in early 2008 (Santschi 2009).[26] In response to the clashes that threatened not only the relations between Dinka Malwal and Misseriya but also the relationship between the North and the South, the *Government of National Unity* (GoNU) and the *Government of Southern Sudan* (GoSS) interceded (Draft Conference Report 2009).

In early 2008, representatives of the GoNU, GoSS, of the states on the border between today's Sudan and South Sudan, the *Sudan Armed Forces* (SAF), the SPLA and traditional authorities met and agreed to start a peace initiative and to

---

[24] The Sudan Armed Forces (SAF) and the GoS armed the *Murahaleen* militia to raid and fight communities in Northern Bahr el-Ghazal (Beswick 1998; Mathok 2010).

[25] Bradbury et al. argued that peace markets "though limited in effect, were more spontaneous, more of a grassroots movement than the people-to-people meetings" (2006: 37).

[26] According to the UNMIS Civilian Affairs Division, the severe armed clashes were attributed to "causing a high number of fatalities on both sides" (UNMIS 2008). Before and after these serious clashes "low-level acts of violence and abuses perpetrated by both sides" occurred.

establish peace committees in both communities (Draft conference report 2009).[27] The peace committees that were formed in community meetings organized reciprocal visits of officials and community representatives and a peace conference. Accordingly, the GoNU, GoSS and the state level governments including educated, senior community members played a pivotal role in the peace process. In that sense the Dinka Malwal-Misseriya peace conference was not part of a 'grassroots' initiative.

The Dinka Malwal-Misseriya peace conference aimed according to the organizers at fostering "reconciliation, stability, reconstruction and sustainable development of Northern Bahr el-Ghazal and Southern Kordofan" (Santschi 2009: 6). The peace conference involved a range of actors including chiefs in addition to youth and women representatives from both communities, government officials from Southern as well as from Northern Sudan. Chiefs made up the majority of the participants. Furthermore, representatives of neighbouring states, foreign governments and international agencies attended the conference. International agencies and bilateral partners supported the conference.

After Christian and Islamic prayers, speeches by officials, elders and international representatives followed. Part of the speeches underlined the commonalities, interdependence and relatedness of the two communities including similar livelihood systems, intermarriages and kinship ties and neighbourhood and referred to previously good relations and the significance of peaceful coexistence (Santschi 2009). Common interests such as trade and development were mentioned as well. Other speakers were more critical and related to past clashes and alleged arming of Misseriya by SAF and the National Congress Party (NCP).

Topics discussed at the conference comprised, among others, grazing movements, security and disarmament of Misseriya herders migrating with their cattle into the territory of Northern Bahr el-Ghazal State, the return of Dinka Malwal abductees, the opening of the road in addition to issues related to the development of the two states (Johnson 2010). The participants agreed on a number of issues including on "access to water and grazing land in the dry season, on the return of abducted women and children, on compensation for persons killed or made to 'disappear', on destroyed property and on disarmament in accordance with the CPA" (Santschi 2009: 6). However, such recommendations were not binding and not all of them were implemented. Joint courts were for instance not established and many abductees were not returned (Concordis International 2012).

Some topics including the arming of Misseriya herders, narratives on the past clashes and the abduction of Dinka Malwal children and women were contested and members of the two groups portrayed conflicting interests and views. However, the most contentious aspects related to national level issues; thus, the border demarcation, the deployment of armed forces and militias as well as the disputed

[27] Senior politicians from both areas were part of the committee. In addition to that, a GoNU ministerial committee under the senior SPLM member Pagan Amum and the senior NCP official Ahmed Haroun oversaw the peace process (Draft conference report 2009).

Abyei area, were deliberately omitted from the conference agenda (Santschi 2009). Accordingly, similar to the Wunlit peace conference, the Dinka Malwal-Misseriya conference did not address points of contention between GoS and GoSS. A number of participants stressed that points of contention affecting the national, now international, level such as the demarcation of the contested border cannot be addressed by inter-communal meetings. Although the inter-communal dimension of the conflict in the case of the Dinka Malwal and Misseriya cannot be separated from international bones of contention such as the border demarcation, inter-communal conferences cannot deal with these causes of conflict.[28]

Despite the unresolved issues, the border between Northern Bahr el-Ghazal and South Kordofan was already reopened due to the peace initiative in April 2008. As a consequence, transhumance activities were possible, trade resumed and serious hostilities between the SPLA and Misseriya at least temporarily halted. At the 2008 peace conference, a representative of a donor agency stressed the importance of development and service provision in relation to peacemaking. This and other agencies supported infrastructure development and service delivery in both states.

Further peace conferences between Dinka Malwal and Misseriya took place for instance in early 2012 and 2013. In addition, smaller scale training workshops and meetings were held with the support of international NGOs. One example is a meeting that was organized by the State Peace Commission in partnership with the *United States Institute of Peace* (USIP) and the support of USAID/AECOM (*Architecture, Engineering, Consulting, Operations and Maintenance*) in July 2010. During this workshop, participants stressed for instance that both sides would not follow and prosecute livestock thieves. Further challenges discussed were the disarmament of Misseriya in addition to thefts and abuses by members of the SPLA (USIP 2010). Accordingly, peace conferences do not necessarily solve challenges such as the impunity of theft by members of armed forces such as the SPLA and SAF and other criminal acts (USIP 2010).

Misseriya pastoralists crossed the border to Northern Bahr el-Ghazal with their livestock up to 2010/2011. Yet, in the light of tensions between North and South the border between Sudan and South Sudan was officially closed between 2011 and March/April 2013. As a result of the closing, prices for sorghum, petrol and other goods skyrocketed in Northern Bahr el-Ghazal and other states bordering Sudan negatively affecting the livelihood of inhabitants of the northern part of South Sudan. In addition to that, Misseriya pastoralists did not cross the border to South Sudan in 2011/2012 due to "persistent suspicion between the two communities and a wider deterioration in security" (Concordis International 2012: 24).[29] Accordingly, the

[28] Respondents from Northern Bahr el-Ghazal argued that the NCP tried to influence the conference. The respondents assumed that the NCP had no interest in good relations between Dinka Malwal and Misseriya (Santschi 2009).

[29] Yet, the relations between Rizeiqat from Darfur, who enter the north-western parts of Northern Bahr el-Ghazal for grazing whereas the Misseriya herders move to the north-eastern part of Northern Bahr el-Ghazal, were better. Accordingly, the Rizeiqat continue to move their livestock to Northern Bahr el-Ghazal (Concordis International 2012).

relations between Misseriya and Dinka Malwal are strongly influenced by national political processes and tensions between Sudan and South Sudan.

The example of the Dinka Malwal-Misseriya peace process exemplifies similarly to the Wunlit peace conference that these 'local' peace processes and conferences involve numerous stakeholders including government actors and are supported by international agencies. In addition, the example illustrates that 'local' peace conferences are strongly influenced and can be hampered by national and international political tensions. Accordingly, cross-border 'local' peace processes have a national and international dimension and are not solely confined to the 'local' sphere. It is therefore hardly possible to delink local level peace processes from national political developments. Last but not least, Dinka Malwal-Misseriya peace conferences do not solely aim at settling disputes but they are part and parcel of yearly negotiations over access to pasture and water. In that sense they are not conclusive but continuing.

4.4 Conclusions

As illustrated above, chiefs play a pivotal role in local justice provision as they try the large majority of intra-communal disputes that are brought to court in South Sudan. Whereas intra-communal conflicts are mostly solved in informal or formal local arenas of justice, inter-communal conflicts—and in particular armed inter-communal conflicts—that affect larger communities and different ethnic groups are addressed in other conflict resolution forums such as special courts, inter-communal meetings as well as peace and reconciliation processes. Yet, local justice and conflict resolution mechanisms are strongly intertwined in South Sudan. Chiefs try cases and at the same time are also involved in peace processes. Furthermore, with their engagement in local justice, chiefs settle disputes that if unsolved may destabilize communities and cause intra- as well as inter-communal violence.

'Local' conflict resolution mechanisms are not solely confined to traditional authorities and to the local level, i.e. to county, payam and bomas. The government and state institutions including the military since the colonial era up to the present day have played an important role in 'local' peace processes and peace conferences since the colonial era up to the present day. The success of the Wunlit peace conference is partly ascribed to the fact that diverse stakeholders including the SPLM/A and other militia groups have been involved in it. At the same time 'local' peace processes are strongly intertwined with and influenced by national political processes. In addition to that, external actors such as UNMISS, donors and international agencies and NGOs support peace initiatives and peace conferences. Such external support includes among other things financial and logistical assistance and facilitation services by external actors.

Abbreviations

AECOM	Architecture, Engineering, Consulting, Operations and Maintenance
CBO	Community Based Organization
CPA	Comprehensive Peace Agreement
GoNU	Government of National Unity
GoS	Government of Sudan
GoSS	Government of Southern Sudan until July 9 2011, after independence of South Sudan Government of South Sudan
IGAD	Inter-Governmental Authority on Development
IDP	Internally Displaced Person
NCP	National Congress Party
NGO	Non-Governmental Organization
NSCC	New Sudan Council of Churches
SAF	Sudan Armed Forces
SPLM	Sudan People's Liberation Movement
SPLA	Sudan People's Liberation Army
UNDP	United Nations Development Programme
UNICEF	United Nations Children's Fund
UNMISS	United Nations Mission in South Sudan
USAID	United States Agency for International Development
USIP	United States Institute of Peace

References

Agwanda, Titus; Harris, Geoff, 2009: "People-to-People Peacemaking and Peacebuilding: A Review of the Work of the New Sudan Council of Churches", in: *African Security Review*, 18, 2: 42–52.

Beswick, Stephanie, 1998: "Violence, Ethnicity and Political Consolidation in South Sudan: A History of the Dinka and Their Relations with Their Neighbors" (Ph.D., Michigan State University).

Beyna, Larry S.; Lund, Michael; Stacks, Stacy S.; Tuthill, Janet; Vondal, Patricia, 2001: *The Effectiveness of Civil Society Initiatives in Controlling Violent Conflicts and Building Peace: A Study of Three Approaches in the Greater Horn of Africa. Synthesis Report on Key Findings and Lessons for Improving Practice* (Washington: Management Systems International).

Bradbury, Mark; Ryle, John; Medley, Michael; Sansculotte-Greenidge, Kwesi, 2006: *Local Peace Processes in Sudan: A Baseline Study* (London, Nairobi: Rift Valley Institute).

Concordis, International, 2012: *Crossing the Line: Transhumance in Transition. Along the Sudan-South Sudan Border* (Concordis International).

Deng, Francis Mading, 2011: "Customary Law in the Cross Fire of Sudan's War of Identities", in: Isser, Deborah (Ed.): *Customary Justice and the Rule of Law in War-Torn Societies* (Washington: US Institute of Peace Press): 285–323.

Golooba-Mutebi, Frederick; Mapuor, Adak Costa, 2005: *Traditional Authorities in South Sudan: Chieftainship in the Bahr El Ghazal Region* (Juba: UNDP).

GoSS (Government of Southern Sudan), 2009: *Local Government Act* (Juba: Government of Southern Sudan, GoSS).

Harragin, Simon, 2007: *Waiting for Pay-Day: Anthropological Research on Local-Level Governance Structures in South Sudan* (Save the Children UK).

Höhne, Markus, 2008: *Traditional Authorities and Local Government in Southern Sudan* (Halle/Saale: Max Planck Institute for Social Anthropology).

Jenner, Hadley 2000: *'When Truth Is Denied, Peace Will Not Come': The People-to-People Peace Process of the New Sudan Council of Churches* (Cambridge: Reflecting on Peace Practice Project).

Johnson, Douglas H., 1986: "Judicial Regulation and Administrative Control: Customary Law and the Nuer, 1898–1954", in: *The Journal of African History*, 27, 1: 59–78.

Johnson, Douglas H., 2010: *When Boundaries Become Borders: The Impact of Boundary-Making in Southern Sudan's Frontier Zones* (London, Nairobi: Rift Valley Institute).

Jok, Aleu Akechak; Leitch, Robert A; Vandewint, Carrie, 2004: *A Study of Customary Law in Contemporary Southern Sudan* (Washington D.C.: World Vision International and the South Sudan Secretariat of Legal and Constitutional Affairs).

Kocjok, Dut Majak 1990: *The Northern Bahr Al-Ghazal: People, Alien Encroachment and Rule, 1856-1956* (Santa Barbara: University of California).

Leonardi, Cherry; Leben, Nelson Moro; Santschi, Martina; Isser, H. Deborah, 2010: *Local Justice in Southern Sudan* (Eashington, D.C.: United States Institute of Peace (USIP); London: Rift Valley Institute).

Lienhardt, R. Godfrey, 2003: *Divinity and Experience. The Religion of the Dinka* (Oxford: Clarendon Press).

Local Government Board, 2011: *PeaceBuilding and Conflict Prevention. Peace Resolutions and Plans of Action Year 2011* (Juba: Local Government Board).

Mathok, Dhieu Wol 2010: *Politics of Ethnic Discrimination in Sudan: A Justification for the Secession of South Sudan* http://www.gurtong.net/ECM/Editorial/tabid/124/ctl/ArticleView/mid/519/articleId/4581/Politics-of-Ethnic-Discrimination-in-Sudan-A-Justification-for-the-Secession-of-South-Sudan.aspx.

Mawson, ANM, 1989: *The Triumph of Life: Political Dispute and Religious Ceremonial among the Agar Dinka* (Cambridge: Darwin College).

Mennen, Tiernan 2008: *Adapting Restorative Justice Principles to Reform Customary Courts in Dealing with Gender-Based Violence in Southern Sudan* (San Francisco: DPK Consulting for UNFPA).

Santschi, Martina, 2009: *Report: Dinka Malual - Misseryia Peace Conference 11–14 November 2008, Aweil, Southern Sudan* (Bern: swisspeace).

Santschi, Martina, 2014: "Negotiating Authority and Statehood in Northern Bahr El-Ghazal. (Upcoming Ph.D. Thesis, Bern: University of Bern, Institute of Social Anthropolog, unpublished).

Survey, Small Arms, 2012: *My Neighbour, My Enemy: Inter-Tribal Violence in Jonglei* (Geneva: Small Arms Survey).

UNMIS (United Nations Mission in Sudan), 2008: *Conflict Summary: Misseriiya- Spla* (Khartoum: UNMIS Civilian Affairs Division).

USIP (United States Institute of Peace), 2010: "Dinka/Misseriya Dialogue for Peaceful Coexistence" (Washington, D,C: United States Institute of Peace (USIP), unpublished).

Van Cutsem, Chantal; Galand, Renaud, 2007: *Equal Access to Justice in Southern Sudan: Assessment Report* (Brussels: Avocats Sans Frontières – Brussels: RCN Justice & Démocratie).

Other Literature

Anonymous, 2009: "Draft Conference Report 2009: Proceedings of the Dinka Malual—Misseryia Grassroots Peace Conference" (Juba: Anonymous, unpublished).

An executive chief in his court in Aweil East County, South Sudan. *Source* Martina Santschi/swisspeace. The permission to publish this photograph was granted.

Chapter 5
Maximizing the Potential of Locally Led Peacebuilding in Conflict Affected States

Carolyn Hayman

Abstract There is growing recognition that effective peacebuilding requires the integration of the work of local and external organizations. This chapter argues that there is more capacity within local organizations than is often recognized, using as an example a community based DDR programme in Eastern DRC, which performed well compared with similar programmes led from outside. The importance of local peacebuilding organizations is emphasized in complexity theory, which argues that as conflict is inherently unpredictable, it should be a high priority to strengthen the ability of local organizations and networks to respond quickly to emerging conflict. The article discusses some of the most common dilemmas faced by international organizations wishing to work more collaboratively with local organizations, and ends with recommendations for donors, international NGOs and local NGOs to achieve greater local leadership in peacebuilding.

Keywords Peacebuilding · Local leadership · DDR · DRC · Conflict · Capacity

5.1 Introduction

Every society possesses its own capacity to resolve conflict without using force. If this were not the case, societies would be ungovernable wildernesses. Instead, we see islands of peace even where stronger forces are making determined efforts to stir up violence and antagonism.

Peace Direct has, for the last eight years, sought out the most effective local peacebuilding organizations in various conflict areas, and funded their work, to the best of our ability, always being led by their ideas about what will be most

C. Hayman (✉)
Peace Direct, London, United Kingdom
e-mail: carolyn@peacedirect.org

S. Hellmüller and M. Santschi (eds.), *Is Local Beautiful?*,
SpringerBriefs in Environment, Security, Development and Peace 11,
DOI: 10.1007/978-3-319-00306-1_5, © The Author(s) 2014

effective in that particular situation. This chapter provides a brief case study of one of Peace Direct's partners, the *Centre Résolution Conflits* (CRC), in the Democratic Republic of Congo (DRC). It then sets out a general categorization of the purposes of such locally led peacebuilding work and describes how the CRC fits within this framework. Thirdly, it suggests how external organizations, including funders, can get the most out of their partnerships with local peacebuilding organizations, and avoid damaging precisely those qualities that make them most valuable. Finally, the chapter introduces the concept of Local First, a development approach that looks first for local capacity for action, before bringing in external resources and expertise, which recognizes that much of this capacity is found outside central government and which understands that local people need to lead their own development.

5.2 Overview of the Centre Résolution Conflits

After 15 years of conflict in DRC, many of the estimated 5 million people living in North Kivu continue to suffer on a daily basis and consequently have lost trust in the capacity of their government to resolve the issues facing this part of DRC, which include violent ways of accessing eastern DRC's abundant resources, myriad armed groups, the reintegration of militia groups into the national army, ethnic conflicts, under development, ongoing land disputes and large numbers of *internally displaced persons* (IDPs) and refugees.

Two key challenges to address in states like the DRC are the lack of social cohesion, and the need to restore confidence and links between civilians and their government. Much more than it damages buildings and physical infrastructures, conflict destroys trust and relationships, as well as the capacity and will of people to work together. These intangible qualities must be rebuilt if peace is to be sustainable. Restoring confidence between civilians and governance actors is needed to create forms of cooperation designed to address issues of conflict together. However, in the words of the CRC's current coordinator: "the members of government are another country" (Rouw/Willems 2009).

CRC works across North Kivu and Ituri. The organization has 17 full time staff, a network of part time staff and large numbers of volunteers. Its work is informed at every step by the local population. Currently, it is mainly engaged in four types of activities: negotiations with militia leaders for the return of combatants to the community, including children; preparation of communities to support their return, and that of IDPs, including the development of specialized courts to deal with land disputes; creation of Task Forces that identify and mediate in emerging conflicts before they escalate; and lastly, development of livelihood options that provide an alternative to predation, and enable family formation.

CRC's work in *disarmament, demobilization and reintegration* (DDR) is the subject of a case study "Coming Home" (Gillhespy/Hayman 2011). This study draws attention to the value of the holistic approach that CRC adopts, which is rooted in an understanding of the local context, and tries to break the cycle of exit and re-entry into militia groups which characterizes many movements in Eastern DRC.

By contrast, externally led DDR programmes often have a difficult time connecting with local realities in ways that create sustainable solutions to the threat of armed groups, especially in terms of reintegration issues. However, it is vital to understand "the 'laws of the bush'... in order to break the cycle of returning to the militia. Reintegration must connect to life experienced by the combatants" (Rouw/Willems 2010: 35). Hence CRC plans a DDR process which starts with reintegration—RDD rather than DDR.

Following the sensitization stage, where CRC negotiates with militia leaders for the release of combatants, including children, CRC's approach includes four other key elements. First, the provision of a range of livelihood options, some of which are also open to members of the community. Second, reparation programmes are sometimes included in the reintegration process, whereby former militia members or other families build roads for the benefit of the community. Third, they build social networks based largely on voluntary efforts, which sustains the RDD process at the micro-level over time. Fourth, they have developed context specific indicators that measure success over the long term, and not just at the point where a combatant leaves the militia group and disarms.

This approach succeeds. Through CRC's engagement with (former) combatants before, during and after their RDD work, only 10 per cent of former combatants indicated that they were considering a return to the bush, whereas 58% of former combatants who did not engage with the CRC process indicated that they were considering a return (Gillhespy/Hayman 2011: 21). Relationships have been created that support and protect communities. Peace committees in communities help to organize the cooperatives while six Task Forces, made up of former combatants together with journalists and other community leaders, look out for emerging conflicts and seek to mediate before they lead to violence. 119 radio clubs provide a focus for the initial stages of RDD. As one ex-combatant explains, "I can say I am Kidicho, I have been there with you, now I am here. ... They even cite the name. You, I know you are there, I know you have been shot by the bullet. I know your wife. I know you are living on that mountain. I am already good here, you can come and join me" (Gillhespy/Hayman 2011: 21). Radio is, therefore, a direct way for ex-combatants to encourage their former colleagues to also return to their own communities. In addition, some of the radio clubs have begun community livelihood projects, such as tree nurseries, demonstrating the latent capacity for self-help that communities possess.

CRC works with the *United Nations Organization Stabilization Mission* (MONUSCO) in the DRC, and other international agencies. CRC's local knowledge and accompaniment on MONUSCO's DDR initiatives has prevented misunderstandings that could have led to renewed violence. Without the support of outsiders like UN agencies, however, CRC would have had less leverage with the

Mai–Mai.[1] In particular, the combination of DDR facilities and services provided by the UN and the facilitation of the process by CRC rendered demobilization a more attractive option for militias.

Three main lessons can be drawn from accompanying CRC's work. First, successful RDD programmes require local organizations and external organizations to work together, adopting the roles that each is best suited for. Second, the process of RDD, as opposed to the programme, requires a local presence that can support it over the long term. And third, RDD programmes should be judged by indicators that are seen as relevant by the communities that receive them, not just by the number of weapons collected or participants in the programme.

5.3 Overview of What Local Peacebuilding Work Can Do

This categorization of the different purposes of local peacebuilding work was developed in reaction to the often heard view that "in order to be effective, peacebuilding work has to address the root causes of conflict". This is a great aspiration but in many conflicts, aspects of the political system are root causes, and neither internal nor external organizations can have much impact until an overwhelming pressure for change develops. Hence there is a need also to focus on other aspects of peacebuilding, as shown in the following pyramid, namely on preventing immediate violence, building resilience, and addressing proximate causes (Fig. 5.1).

Aspects of CRC's work fit into all four areas. They stop immediate violence for example through assisting in the disarmament and demobilization of combatants; they address proximate causes of conflict for example through setting up land courts to deal with disputes between returning IDPs and those cultivating their land; they build resilience for example through the creation of Task Forces, bringing together militia commanders (former and in some cases current) army staff, faith leaders, and others, to identify and resolve emerging conflicts, while building trust between Task Force members; and they address root causes for example through developing livelihoods in conflict-affected communities.

Building resilience in communities at risk of repeated violence deserves particular mention. One reason why donors may be reluctant to fund peacebuilding work is the fear that all the impact can be swept away if the political system takes a turn for the worse, or conflict sweeps through a region, as happened in late November 2012 in DRC. However, it is precisely at these moments that communities most need resilience—their response to threat will be heavily conditioned by the degree of trust that has been built up between different sections of the community.

[1] Regional militia groups.

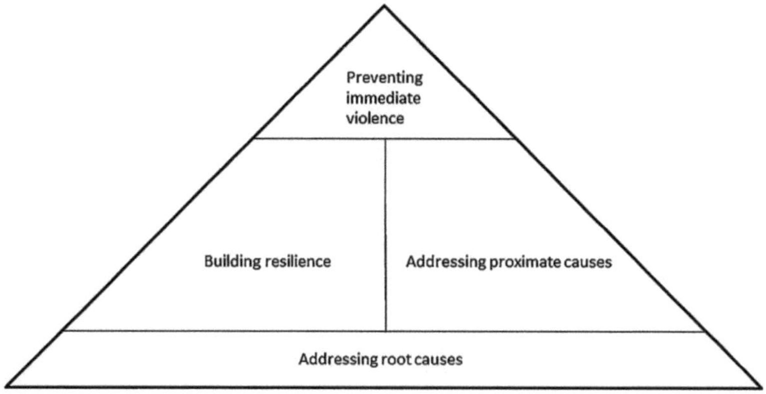

Fig. 5.1 What is local peacebuilding? *Source* www.peacedirect.org (18 October 2013)

Another way of expressing the value of local peacebuilding derives from the 'sparks and field' model of conflict.[2] In this model, the 'field' is the underlying state of society, its propensity to ignite into violent conflict. The 'dryness' of the field could be related to a number of factors—inequality, lack of trust in government, predatory behaviour by security services, lack of livelihoods—and these can to a greater or lesser extent be measured. But the 'spark' that sets the field alight is impossible to predict. The events of 2011 in Tunisia provide a text book example of this.

If the spark cannot be predicted, then it will be important to have a 'bucket of water' to hand at all times, in order to quickly extinguish the spark's ability to create wide scale violence. This does not mean suppressing dissent but rather channelling it into non-violent means. The only organizations that can provide this 'bucket of water' will be those most local to the incident.[3]

[2] See "Leap Confronting Conflict"; at: http://www.leapconfrontingconflict.org.uk/assets-uploaded/documents/pwf-nov2011_1315914192.pdf (18 october 2013).

[3] A more theoretical way of expressing the same consideration is provided by Cedric de Coning (2013), head of the Peace Operations and Peacebuilding Research Group at the *Norwegian Institute of International Affairs* (NUPI): "I have argued that one of the implications of Complexity theory for peacebuilding is that interventions have to be essentially about stimulating and facilitating the capacity of societies to self-organise. The art of peacebuilding thus lies in pursuing the appropriate balance between international support and home-grown context-specific solutions. What is appropriate would depend on the context, however as a general rule of thumb I would argue that international peacebuilding interventions should provide security guarantees that regulate acceptable state behaviour in the international system, and they should stimulate, facilitate and create the space for the emergence of robust and resilient self-organised systems".

5.4 Getting the Most Out of Partnerships with Local Peacebuilding Organizations

International organizations seeking to work in partnership with local peacebuilding organizations need to get away from the prevailing model, whereby a donor or *international non-governmental organization* (INGO) analyses a conflict and decides on the most effective response, and then contracts with a local organization to 'deliver' or 'implement' this response. Instead, outsiders should seek out the most effective local organizations they can find, and support them to carry out their own programmes—which will often, as with CRC's work, adapt and develop in the light of experience. However, working with what Peace Direct calls 'locally led peacebuilding' presents a number of challenges. The rest of the chapter sets these out and suggests some solutions.

5.4.1 Dilemmas

Finding and Assessing Local Capacity

Finding and assessing local capacity to act on a particular issue requires specialist knowledge and experience—from a donor's field based staff, an INGO or a local entity such as a Chamber of Commerce or network.

Organizations need to be judged realistically, by what they have achieved in often challenging circumstances, with limited resources, and against their own objectives. Where organizations claim to be working for community benefit, their legitimacy needs to be tested. Interviewing 'beneficiaries' may not work when people feel that their answers will determine whether badly needed resources are to be provided. A better test may be the extent to which an organization mobilizes voluntary effort. People don't give their time to an organization which they do not feel is working in their interests.

This is a far cry from a call for tenders to be completed in a highly complex form, often in the applicant's second or third language, which have been criticized as favouring 'NGO businesses' specialising in bid writing. There is a place for open competition, but it should be supplemented by other forms of assessment by people with an in-depth knowledge of the field.

Supporting Without Distorting

Generally where local organizations receive external funding, it is in order to scale up their operations. This needs care, if it is not to destroy the qualities that made the organization successful in the first place. Masooda Bano's (2012) chastening account of how external funding destroyed functioning civil society organizations in Pakistan, also draws a sharp distinction between voluntary organizations and NGOs. Voluntary organizations engage volunteer effort, operate with a low cost base, and show long term commitment to their mission and their community. NGOs don't have volunteers, have a cost base more in line with INGOs, and take on the work that someone will fund. Turning a voluntary organization into an NGO is unhelpful.

The example of CRC lines up with Bano's analysis in showing how organizations can grow considerably in scale, as well as employ a team of paid staff, without losing their ability to mobilize voluntary effort. This is a function of how they engage with outside funders. CRC was first of all a pre-existing organization, which had been created in response to a need, not a funding opportunity. Moreover, the organization began with a voluntary self-help ethos and sought funding and partnership on its own terms while limiting the rewards to paid staff.

Bano's recommendations (2012: 175ff) about how to avoid destroying organizations through external funding include: to not pay high salaries to initiators as these sap both their motivation and that of their followers; to fund material activities that benefit the whole organization; to monitor performance in terms of members' satisfaction and engagement; to be willing to work with organizations on equal terms, listening to their perspectives and approaches to development and to adjust incentives over time as the work develops.

Working at Scale

It takes time for organizations to get to a size where they match the scale at which donors prefer to fund. The increasing emphasis on showing impact also tends to work in favour of large scale projects. Almost always, external contractors, or multilateral agencies, are seen as the only organizations able to bid for work at the largest scale.

Yet it is at this scale that prioritising the use of local capacity could have the biggest long term impact. Donors, who genuinely want to prioritize locally led initiatives, will find ways to support groupings of organizations who collectively can deliver at scale. For example, the community based DDR work described in the case study of the CRC could be carried out, with support from CRC, by a number of other organizations based across North Kivu. Rather than demobilising 4,300 combatants and reintegrating 1,300, a consortium could work with five times or even ten times this number.

Redefining Roles

Even if donor governments could be persuaded of the benefits of supporting locally led peacebuilding, would recipient governments accept it? Would the trade-off of greater use of local capacity, and a greater role for recipient governments in shaping their own contribution, compensate for the possible loss of access to aid funds and the prestige that comes from deploying those funds? Can desire to provide better public goods be harnessed? The enthusiasm for the post-Busan New Deal for building peaceful states suggests that the principle of involving civil society more closely in a coherent national plan for peacebuilding is gaining acceptance among governments, though with some notable exceptions.

Multilaterals will continue to have a big role to play. As the case of CRC demonstrates, their access to resources, technical expertise and logistical capacity can be invaluable to their local partners. But they need to be genuinely doing things that could not be done by one or more local organizations. Good examples of partnership need to be encouraged, for example the principle of co-design of projects with local partners.

Working in a locally led way also represents a challenge for INGOs. There will certainly continue to be a role for them, but it may be a changing one—less an implementer, deliverer of standalone capacity building programmes and conduit for donor funds, and more a discoverer and nurturer of talent, with a very clear objective of enabling organizations to lead from the beginning, and to contribute their knowledge to the INGO and its other partners.

5.5 'Local First' as a Means of Encouraging Behaviour Change

Local First attempts to define behaviour changes that will unambiguously embed a different way of working with local organizations. It applies as much to peacebuilding as to other areas of development—possibly even more, as trust is such an essential ingredient in peacebuilding, and it is hard for outsiders to engender trust from a standing start.[4]

This final section suggests some behaviour changes that different players in the field might adopt. Clearly incentives for different organizations also need to change or be reinterpreted—however where there is a recognition that success depends on more effective engagement of local organizations in leadership roles, then by describing specific behaviours that would be likely to achieve this result, it may be possible to lower the barriers to creating change.

5.5.1 Suggestions for Donors

Adapt your approach to capacity assessment, and ensure that the assessment includes the motivation of organizations as well as their effectiveness.

---

[4] The book 'Local First: Development for the twenty-first century' (McGuinness 2012) makes the case for this approach, and illustrates it with six case studies drawn from Africa and Asia.

From a *Local First* perspective, current approaches to capacity assessment have three limitations:

- *We assess needs but not capacity.*
  If a needs assessment is conducted without a parallel capacity assessment that looks at which local institutions at local, state and national level are currently meeting the identified needs, or could do so with additional resources, then almost inevitably external delivery solutions will be sought.
- *We don't have good ways to find capacity in non-traditional places.*
  The capacity to deliver may be found in far-flung places, beyond the capital city, through particularly effective state and local government institutions, through civil society networks[5] or organizations, or in the private sector. Justice is a prime example where in many low income countries, particularly post-conflict and fragile states, a vanishingly small proportion of justice is provided by the formal state sector.
- *We assess capacity against predefined criteria, rather than investigating what organizations are already able to do.*
  The capacity that Local First prioritizes is the capacity for innovation, entrepreneurship—for seeing opportunities and devising effective ways to exploit them, for taking existing local practices and adapting and improving them and above all, for listening to the demands and needs of the population and seeking to meet them.

Commit to using external organizations as a last resort, not a first resort, and as supportive partners to local organizations, not as contractors.

There is considerable inertia in the system and an understandable desire on the part of organizations charged with using public money wisely to continue with tried and tested methods. Hence even with the determination of the Head of USAID to increase the proportion of its resources going directly to local organizations and governments to 30%, the proportion going to US commercial contractors actually went up in 2011.[6]

Donors will need to find new ways of supporting locally led networks and consortia, in order to enable large scale projects to be locally delivered.

Identify a few sectors within which to experiment with a Local First approach and aim over time to target an increasing percentage of funding within those sectors to locally led or locally owned programmes.

Measurable targets are important in forcing change, so it is not surprising that these are increasingly being mentioned as a way of shifting the emphasis towards a Local First approach. As well as the USAID target mentioned above, the UK

---

[5] For descriptions of civil society networks in many environmental fields operating at a large scale, for an example of how this could work in relation to land registration, see Bigg and Satterthwaite (2005).

[6] Source: www.foreignpolicy.com/articles/2012/07/18/hired_gun_fight (1 october 2013).

International Development Committee recently recommended that 10 per cent of UK aid to DRC should go to local organizations.

Targets could also be applied equally to the procurement of goods and services from the commercial sector, and to the use of NGOs to provide services in sensitive areas such as justice, security and accountability—sectors where a stronger civil society presence is also likely to improve government performance, as the case studies indicate.

Commit to long term evaluations of impact, sustainability and value for money from the locally led versus the internationally led projects.

It is hard to compare value for money and impact in projects where local and international efforts are closely intertwined. Nevertheless, if Local First is an idea worth testing, then evaluations need to be able to discern to what extent programmes are genuinely locally led.

Success or failure needs to be viewed over at least a five year time frame, and capture impact that goes beyond what was specified at the outset (for example in the log frame), in order to assess the added value of having locals working as principals not just as agents. And the sustainability of the work that has been set in train needs to be assessed, after the programme ends, and checked out several years later.

Enable structures that will allow local organizations to scale up their impact.

Commitment to Local First will recognize that consistent funding is needed if local organizations are going to be able to run programmes at the same scale as multilaterals and INGOs. Local organizations, as they scale up, will need funding and possibly support with core functions such as finance, governance and measurement of impact.

Ensure that evaluations include an assessment of the impact of the project on the growth or decline in local capacity.

In the UK government's recent, extremely thorough, review of multilateral organizations, the organizations were judged against 41 criteria (DfID 2011). None of the criteria referred to the organization's success in transferring responsibility to local organizations. If the ultimate goal of aid is for countries to graduate from receiving it in order to be self-reliant, then every programme should have explicit goals about the extent to which, at the end of the programme, local organizations, whether public sector, private sector or non-profit, have taken over aspects of delivery.

5.5.2 Suggestions for INGOs

Evaluate in what ways organizational practice is locally led or locally owned, and how this can be demonstrated.

Anyone working in development must surely see their ultimate goal as to have empowered people to do their own development and become self-reliant.

Therefore, all development organizations should consider how their ways of working reflect Local First values, and how they would demonstrate this. The *Local First* community of practice (www.localfirst.org.uk) is being developed to support new ways of working.

Set a goal to increase the Local First orientation of our work, and define how this increase can be demonstrated.

A second step is to look for areas of improvement and set some goals. For example, this could be a goal to directly channel a greater percentage of funds to local organizations, rather than through the organization's local staff, or to ensure that all evaluations measure the extent to which responsibility and capacity has been transferred to the local partner.

Seek out local suppliers of goods and services, including audit, market research and evaluation.

A concerted move by INGOs to use services such as audit, market research and evaluation from local suppliers would help to create employment locally, as well as having other benefits—for example, local evaluation staff can travel to areas out of bounds to international staff.

5.5.3 Suggestions for Local NGOs

Seek funding and support on the organization's own terms, and resist being cast as delivery agents.

Local organizations face difficult choices when they are asked by funders to deliver programmes that they believe to be sub-optimal, or even likely to fail. Taking on the contract ensures the organization survives and may enable it to keep its own programmes going, but risks tarnishing the organization's reputation. Local organizations should at the least remain very clear about why they are undertaking a particular piece of work, and maintain their ability to set their own priorities.

Maintain the involvement of the wider community as volunteers, and ensure that the organization has a survival strategy in the absence of external funding.

Local organizations that want to scale up their impact need to safeguard their ability to continue to operate in the absence of funding from international sources. Funders can be fickle, more often facing constraints of their own that work against long term funding relationships, while host governments may impose restrictions on funding from outside the country. Hence local organizations need to cultivate local sources of funding and have in mind a strategy to safeguard the capacity they have put in place, where possible through generating local funds.

Remunerate paid staff in keeping with local wage rates.

Local organizations that look to the long term need to safeguard their ability to mobilize volunteer effort and to have a wage structure that is sustainable. Both require salaries to retain a relationship with local wages.

Seek to connect community based activity with local and national government, as well as with the work of INGOs and multilaterals, in order to coordinate with and influence them.

Local organizations need to play their part in achieving a degree of coordination between their work and the initiatives of multilaterals, and local and national governments. They have valuable insights to contribute, and their work will be easier and more effective if these insights inform the work of other players.

The Local First community of practice is being developed to support new ways of working that reflect the values of Local First.

References

Bano, Masooda, 2012: *Breakdown in Pakistan—How aid is eroding institutions for collective action* (Standord: Stanford University Press).

Bigg, Tom; Satterthwaite, David (Eds.), 2005: *How to Make Poverty History: the central role of local organisations in meeting the MDGs* (London: International Institute for Environment and Development).

De Coning, Cedric, 2013: ‘‘Complexity theory and the local in peacebuilding’’; at: http://www.insightonconflict.org/2013/06/complexity-theory-and-the-local-in-peacebuilding/ (30 September 2013).

DfID, 2011: *Multilateral Aid Review* (London: DfID). at: http://www.dfid.gov.uk/Documents/publications1/mar/multilateral_aid_review.pdf (30 September 2013).

Gillhespy, Tom; Hayman, Carolyn, 2011: *Coming Home: A case study of community led Disarmament, Demobilization and Reintegration in D.R. Congo* (London: Peace Direct).

McGuinness, Kate (Ed.), 2012: *Local First: Development for the twenty-first century* (London: Peace Direct).

Rouw, Hans; Willems, Rens C., 2009: unpublished field notes.

Rouw, Hans; Willems, Rens C., 2010: *Connecting Community Security and DDR: Experiences from Eastern DRC* (The Hague: Peace Security and Development Network).

Traditional Dance Ceremony at a Peace Day, Berunda, DR Congo. *Source* Sara Hellmüller/swisspeace. The permission to publish this photo was granted.

Chapter 6
Peacebuilding: Switzerland's Approach to Local Ownership

Ambassador Claude Wild

Abstract Questions of local ownership are unavoidable and fundamental in post-conflict peacebuilding processes. They need to be approached in the best interests of the peace process and sustainable peacebuilding solutions. An international approach to local ownership thus means that external actors are required to carefully assess the needs of internal actors and to be ready to review their own roles. Switzerland is committed to not exporting preconceived solutions to any country or region and to include difficult partners in its actions. Overall, Swiss endeavours aim for local ownership to go beyond an engagement of local populations in outside driven processes. Rather, they focus on allowing locals to develop their activities and take responsibility for domestically driven peacebuilding processes with outside support. Switzerland wants to play an enabling role by identifying and supporting local actors who have the credibility and the willingness to assume responsibility for their country's future. Peacebuilding can only succeed with the sustained contribution and commitment of both internationals and locals.

Keywords Switzerland · Local ownership · Glocal · Peacebuilding · Capacity development · Post-conflict · Mediation

6.1 Introduction

International donors face several dilemmas when trying to engage in a given local context. The specificity of each country and region makes it impossible to coherently follow political guidelines and general sets of principles, norms, rules,

---

Ambassador C. Wild (✉)
Head of the Human Security Division at the Swiss Federal Department of Foreign Affairs, Bern, Switzerland

S. Hellmüller and M. Santschi (eds.), *Is Local Beautiful?*,
SpringerBriefs in Environment, Security, Development and Peace 11,
DOI: 10.1007/978-3-319-00306-1_6,

and practices established in capital cities. Nevertheless, questions of local ownership are unavoidable and fundamental in post-conflict peacebuilding processes. They need to be approached in the best interests of the peace process and sustainable peacebuilding solutions. An international approach to local ownership thus means that external actors are required to carefully assess the needs of beneficiaries and be ready to review their own roles. The modalities of how strategic advice and capacity building are provided are important.

This article is shaped around the question of how Switzerland, as a donor and as an actor in the field of peacebuilding and human security, stimulates and enables local ownership. The first part discusses the fact that peacebuilding concepts must be designed, discussed and implemented by locals in order to be effective. It provides a definition that Switzerland applies when it talks about local ownership in peacebuilding. The subsequent section discusses the dilemmas when it comes to identifying local partners. It establishes that choices are not always easy and demand some degree of flexibility and re-thinking by international actors. The article continues by illustrating some of the guiding principles of Swiss engagement considering local contexts and multiple actors. The article concludes with some concrete examples of how Switzerland engages with locals in various contexts.

6.2 Local Ownership in Peacebuilding: What Does it Mean?

Locals and internationals/donors might have different motivations and therefore find themselves often at different ends of what should be seen as a common action. Although most of the stakeholders agree upon the need for local ownership, the question of how to ensure local buy-in and sustainability is not always easy to answer, as the meaning and the practice of local ownership do not always result in the same action and outcome. In theory, local ownership is accepted, but it is not always practiced generally and with all actors and equally across the board. This leads to the perception that local ownership automatically creates a situation of *insider* and *outsider*.

Local ownership is not when domestic actors buy into what remains an externally defined vision. It refers to the extent to which domestic actors are included in and ideally also control both the design and implementation of political and peace processes. Peacebuilding concepts must be designed, managed and implemented by local actors rather than by external donors. In post-conflict contexts, this implicitly suggests that peace processes, which are not embraced by local actors, are likely to fail. In the field of its peacebuilding activities, Switzerland defines local ownership as the capacity to "enable local actors to design and lead a process, to lead an initiative, or to be in a position of influence, in the context of the peacebuilding efforts which are undertaken in their societal environment". According to this definition, the concept of *being affected* defines actors as *being local.*

6.3 Partners and Spoilers: The Agony of Choice

While there exists common understanding that local ownership is important and needs to be considered, the decision of with whom to work is not always as obvious as one would assume. An international donor often faces the difficulty of identifying appropriate local partners. Not every context provides an obvious candidate. Pressing needs may require engaging in a dialogue and partnership with less desirable, but still influential partners. It may also be the case that internationals need to engage with 'difficult' local actors, in particular when these actors exercise control over significant parts of the territory and the population. In that case, they need to be taken into account as partners because if they are excluded, they may well spoil national and/or international efforts for building peace. Hence they need to be engaged and brought on board as part of the solution.

Thus, it is obvious that in order to achieve peace, various stakeholders need to be included in efforts for peacebuilding. This counts as much for private actors as for politicians and community leaders. Local actors include a variety of stakeholders from government representatives, civil society groups, affected populations (such as victims), opposition groups, national and provincial politicians, community, business and religious leaders, victims associations, academics, artists etc. However, local actors in a globalized world are not a homogenous group and rarely do they speak with one voice.

In order to be successful, local ownership needs to be promoted at various degrees, at various stages, and across the entire spectrum of activities. Over the years, the interlocutors have shifted and expanded. For example with increased globalization multinational corporations operating in certain areas can become local actors who need to be taken into account. The activities of multinational corporations together with their local branches are influential and deserve the donor's attention in certain contexts. This illustrates that it is not always possible to draw a clear line between global and local actors and reality on the ground is characterized by actions coming from a *glocal* political context (see Box 6.1).

An important aspect when engaging local interlocutors is to target those stakeholders that are perceived as legitimate actors by the locals themselves, and not just by the donor country. Determining who is *local* and *legitimate* therefore requires good context analysis and knowledge.

Donors do not only face the difficult choice of working together with spoilers or illegitimate local actors. Often internationals are confronted with a choice between *effectiveness* (i.e. work with those who hold the most power) and *legitimacy* (i.e. work with those who have the best international standing or the greatest public support), or choosing a partner with the most *capacity*. External actors have a tendency to look for 'like-minded' partners when they are searching for local ownership. However, like-minded partners might lack legitimacy and effectiveness in the area where they act. Therefore, one approach is to select local actors who can serve as effective partners, independent from the fact of whether they are like-minded or not.

When choosing local partners one also has to consider choosing between the national elite and the general public. The first, and for many people logical choice, might be to work with the national elite only. It is true that the general public is rarely a homogenous group of people. It is rather composed of heterogeneous fractions of society. This renders the choice difficult. The choice of the actor might be conditioned by the environment international actors want to work in. When working in central urban settings, the choice of engaging with the national elite might be obvious. However if one wants to work in less urban and more rural environments, an engagement with community based, non-elite actors, is necessary.

International actors need to secure local ownership, but also need to build on existing institutions and thus take local contexts into consideration. Problems need to be seen in a more nuanced and context specific way. Sustainable peace should not be built by outsiders. They should be there to interact *with* local counterparts rather than act *on* local counterparts. This leads to a more coherent peacebuilding approach which encloses facilitations, mediation and conflict resolution.

Box 6.1 GLOCAL political context
The choice and link between international engagement and local ownership is not an either-or decision. In many instances no clear line between the global and the local context and actors can be drawn. As soon as one acts in a peacebuilding paradigm, the area could easily be identified as being *glocal.* The glocal arena couples the actions of local stakeholders on the ground together with activities of international donors. Both areas are connected and influenced by each other. The glocal lenses take into account the varying dynamics and differing logics of the arenas where the competing norms and claims of global, regional, national and local actors are being negotiated and dealt with. Glocal relationships are complex since actions of various actors overlap on the ground.

6.4 Swiss Engagement: Guiding Principles

Switzerland has a long standing tradition of engagement in the fields of peacebuilding and human rights and has had several experiences in peace process design. It is therefore considered by many as a trustworthy partner in these fields. This reputation has also emerged because Switzerland's actions are based on a number of guiding principles which consider local contexts and multiple actors.

Switzerland is committed to not exporting preconceived solutions to any country or region. For many years, Switzerland has been working with *Human Security Advisors* (HSA) in the regions and countries of its engagement. HSAs are in the midst of the field and can provide a good context analysis. While doing so, they look for potential local actors with whom Switzerland can and wants to engage in order to encourage durable solutions to human security problems. Currently Switzerland deploys about 20 HSAs in various regions.

Another important guiding principle is that difficult partners are not excluded from Switzerland's actions. As previously mentioned, in order to engage in local ownership, one needs to work with difficult partners. Switzerland sees the need to engage spoilers, non-state actors, the business community, religious groups or those motivated by faith which, at first instance, can be perceived as 'illegitimate' by some actors.

This does not undermine Switzerland's conviction that local actors need to respect a set of common standards to which Switzerland has subscribed in its national and foreign policy actions. This includes that local partners respect universal values such as *jus cogens*, International Humanitarian Law, and Human Rights Law. This engagement also applies to businesses based in Switzerland with important branches in other countries. Switzerland is home to some of the most important multinational commodity and energy companies in the world. They, too, have a responsibility to respect human rights and the environment. Switzerland is working to ensure that companies accept this responsibility and not only observe international standards of corporate governance but also engage in sectoral voluntary multi-stakeholder institutions on corporate social responsibility. Therefore, Switzerland works closely together with private companies.

While engaging with local actors, it is also important to consider and include sectors of society which are often in marginalized positions and do not have overall influence in the local context. Examples of such groups include women, children, and ethnic minorities. There is a need for mechanisms to engage with civil society organizations in general and NGOs working on gender issues in particular. In this respect, Switzerland promotes local ownership but also empowerment, especially empowerment of women.

In the contexts of its engagement, Switzerland is supporting south-south and triangular cooperation wherever opportunities arise. This principle contributes to enhancing the knowledge flow between countries from the south which have had similar experiences and can share examples of successful projects. It is important that local capacities are build up as quickly as possible. If governance functions are carried out jointly by international and local actors, then full responsibility should be rapidly transferred into local hands.

Many Swiss peacebuilding activities are bilateral. Nevertheless, Switzerland is also active in many multilateral initiatives. For instance, although Switzerland cannot determine the mandate of peacekeeping operations, because they are mandated by the UN Security Council, Switzerland tries to influence things when mandates are put into practice by bringing in the local dimension.

6.5 Paradigms of Local Ownership: Selected Case Studies of Swiss Engagement and Local Ownership

Mediation in peace processes is one of Switzerland's foreign policy priorities. Mediation plays a vital role in ending armed conflicts and major political crises around the world. While Switzerland has its own competent mediators, it also supports the involvement of regional facilitators and mediators. Sometimes Switzerland entirely withdraws from an active mediation when local or regional actors are ready to overtake leadership. After an engagement of several years in Mali, for example, Switzerland was approached by the Tuareg rebels to mediate between them and the government. Switzerland took on the role, but as soon as the *Economic Community of West African States* (ECOWAS) designated a regional mediator, Switzerland supported this initiative and put itself at the disposal of the mediation activities of Burkina Faso (acting as ECOWAS mediator). While supporting Burkina Faso's work in Mali, Switzerland places itself in the context of the paradigm which suggests that 'African solutions for Africa'—i.e. regional ownership of the mediation process—provide the highest chance for success.

Working with regional or local mediators certainly adds values to international efforts. Following the transition process of 2011, more than 10 cease-fire agreements were concluded in Myanmar. Government officials and insider mediators successfully managed to start the process. As part of its engagement to support the transition process, Switzerland is now helping to build up sufficient local expertise for mediation in Myanmar.

An important challenge in peacebuilding is the (in) existence of local capacities. Switzerland invests important resources in enhancing local capacities. In South Sudan, for example, Switzerland engages with traditional leaders, especially in the rural context. They are empowered in order to guarantee dispute mechanisms where there are no established institutional dispute settlements. In Burundi, Switzerland supports the development of a local platform to build local capacities for holding dialogues among political stakeholders in the run up to the 2015 elections. Providing the capacities to institutionalize such dialogues is one of the ways of linking peacebuilding to statebuilding and of fostering a democratic culture.

Many conflicts are complex and can only find peaceful solutions via an engagement on multiple levels. Contexts of chronic urban violence and political instability have their own paradigm and interventions need to be adapted accordingly. Switzerland places emphasis on engagement on multiple levels with multiple stakeholders. Switzerland's support for Haiti for example includes national, local, but also regional actors from Brazil who are all committed to combating the high level of armed violence. The aim of the project is to increase local capacities for peaceful conflict resolution and to decrease the perceptions of security forces as an additional threat in an environment which is fraught with poverty and violence. The vicious circle of armed conflict can only be broken if the local community takes ownership of the conflict resolution processes and is assisted in developing the necessary resilience. With this project, Switzerland supports south-south cooperation in a fragile context.

Certainly, sometimes projects linked to a peace process do not develop in a way in which Switzerland would ideally design them (according to Swiss standards), but in a way which is shaped by local conditions. In order to be able to support the right local partners, Switzerland can make concessions when supporting local peacebuilding actors and/or solutions. However, concessions are never made on values or principles, such as human rights or the rule of law, but on administrative standards. Local NGOs for example may sometimes find themselves in competition with international NGOs. They may have difficulties providing project proposals which pass high standards set up by international donors who might be tempted to support international NGOs rather than local NGOs. In this situation, Switzerland finds it important to encourage international NGOs to help local NGOs to build up capacities for project proposals. In the case of Switzerland's Human Security Programme in Myanmar, for example, the Embassy of Switzerland in Yangon is providing the documents for local NGOs so they can directly apply for Swiss grants.

6.6 Conclusion

The above description of guiding principles and practical examples illustrates how important a solid anchoring in local communities and politics is, when it comes to peacebuilding activities of international donors. Switzerland wants to play an enabling role by identifying and supporting local actors who have the credibility and the willingness to assume responsibility for their country's future. Peacebuilding can only succeed with the sustained contribution and commitment of both internationals and locals.

For too long there has been a general tendency to overestimate international capacity and to underestimate local/domestic potentials. The international community needs to overcome this false paradigm. Obviously, it does not apply everywhere. But in cases where there is a lack of strong local or domestic partners and potentials, international actors need to provide support in order to create space for building up capacity rather than imposing unsustainable solutions. Donor rhetoric about ownership must match donor actions on the ground and not be undermined by administrative concerns. It is only in this way that local ownership will go beyond an engagement of local populations in outside driven processes. Local ownership should rather be about allowing locals to develop their activities and take responsibility for domestically driven peacebuilding processes with outside support. The time of imposing solutions that are conceived from the outside without local ownership should definitely be over in peacebuilding solutions of the twenty first century. After all, true local ownership of a peacebuilding process means local responsibility for the process.

Participants in a workshop on mediation in the context of elections in Conakry, Guinea. *Source* Mediation Support Project (a joint venture between swisspeace and the Center for Security Studies (CSS, ETH Zurich) funded by the Swiss Federal Department of Foreign Affairs). The permission to use this photo was granted.

Chapter 7
Partners for Peace: A Case Study of Local—International Cooperation

Rachel Gasser and Ja Nan Lahtaw

Abstract After the initiation of a democratic reform process in March 2011, the regime in Myanmar, being challenged by democratic and ethnic-based opposition movements for decades, has started peace negotiations with approximately nineteen armed groups, all of them with different agendas and priorities, even within the groups themselves. The government under president Thein Sein insisted in managing all peace processes without any engagement of a third party mediator. The opening process is also marked by an enormous increase of international stakeholders eager to contribute to a peaceful transition. This influx has had different impacts; on the one hand, the international community has enriched the landscape of local actors and contributed to the process by facilitating contacts, sharing expertise and building capacities; on the other hand, the increased presence is also problematic insofar as it bears the risk of enhancing dependency as well as compromising local ownership and inclusivity. The present case study illustrates the cooperation between the Myanmar NGO Shalom Foundation and the Swiss NGO swisspeace as a successful way of constructive collaboration. By seconding a mediation expert for several months, knowledge exchange and local mediation capacity have been strengthened while guaranteeing local ownership and inclusivity—an innovative way to be replicated.

Keywords Myanmar · Cooperation · Complementarity · Ethnic conflict · Peacebuilding

R. Gasser (✉)
swisspeace, Bern, Switzerland
e-mail: rachel.gasser@swisspeace.ch

J. N. Lahtaw
Shalom (Nyein) Foundation, Yangon, Myanmar
e-mail: janan.shalom@gmail.com

S. Hellmüller and M. Santschi (eds.), *Is Local Beautiful?*,
SpringerBriefs in Environment, Security, Development and Peace 11,
DOI: 10.1007/978-3-319-00306-1_7,

7.1 Introduction: Current State of Play in Myanmar[1]

Over the past 60 years, two different groups of actors have challenged the Myanmar authoritative regime: the democratic opposition movement on the one hand, and various ethnic groups on the other. In the past 18 months the government has exceeded observer expectations by initiating a democratic reform process and starting to engage in ceasefire and peace negotiations with several ethnic armed groups. These processes are moving rapidly and, at the moment, there are approximately 19 different peace processes running in parallel.[2] Currently, all of these peace processes are being managed by one single negotiation team from the government, without the engagement of a third party mediator.

Swift progress has been made in reaching preliminary ceasefire agreements[3] with most ethnic armed groups. However, armed clashes between various sides continue and thus remain an obstacle to achieving sustainable peace. The government also recognizes that broader political dialogue needs to be put in place in addition to the signing of ceasefire agreements, in order to address the underlying grievances and aspirations of ethnic communities. Indeed, the numerous ongoing peace processes with ethnic groups deserve consideration, as a return to violence in the borderlands could derail the current democratic reform process and hinder any meaningful economic and political development in the country.

This chapter explores the new possibilities for peacebuilding initiatives that have come with Myanmar's democratic opening, and will show why local ownership and inclusivity are crucial for Myanmar's peacebuilding process. It will also demonstrate why an inclusive approach in Myanmar is currently difficult to reach, and how international actors may support and complement existing local peace initiatives. The paper will draw on a joint project between swisspeace and the Myanmar organization, the *Nyein (Shalom) Foundation* as an example of a peacebuilding initiative fostering both local ownership and inclusivity. The chapter concludes with a few observations for international actors interested in engagement on the ground.

7.2 Internationals/Nationals: Why Complementarity is Key for Successful Peacebuilding Initiatives

Since Myanmar's democratic opening, the country has been experiencing an influx or a 'gold rush' of international actors who are eager to participate in peacemaking activities. After 60 years of isolation under the military regime, Myanmar

[1] The authors would like to thank Deborah Ferber for her contribution to the text as well as Rina Alluri, Sara Hellmüller, Matthias Siegfried and Mathias Zeller for their critical review.

[2] As of 1 October 2012, according to the *Nyein (Shalom) Foundation*.

[3] These are technically more 'truces' than ceasefire agreements.

now welcomes international support both at a financial and technical level. In this context, an assessment of the possibilities for cooperation between local and international actors at this stage of Myanmar's peace process is crucial. Further it is relevant to reflect on how international actors can give precedence to fostering and preserving local 'agents of change' and their political space.

'Agents of change' can be found at the formal as well as informal level and at the national as well as at the local level, as national actors are those primarily driving and supporting local peace efforts by developing creative models. Reaching an inclusive peace process, however, remains difficult in a setting where different parties' interests are at stake and where parties' priorities on conflict resolution differ. Indeed even the single 'groups' of actors cannot be regarded as a homogeneous entity as individuals within these groups may have different agendas. In this regard, it may be useful for international actors to pay particular attention to the nature, aims, and status of different local actors before supporting peacebuilding initiatives.

The Myanmar government insists on being in the driver's seat of all peace processes, and has envisioned an ambitious three-stage peace process which encompasses ceasefires, economic development, and regional as well as national political dialogue; all to be accomplished by the end of 2015. However, this plan is often revisited and most, if not all, actors now envisage a longer process. The government cannot be deemed a monolithic entity as key reformers such as the president himself and his close adviser and key government negotiator, Minister U Aung Min, have to very carefully protect their space of action. Although the government claims a leading role in the peace processes, it also receives support from the Myanmar think tank *Egress*, and in particular from some of its founding members, to elaborate and conduct the peace negotiations. The *Myanmar Peace Centre*, a quasi-governmental body was created in the fall of 2012 by presidential decree, and is the main coordinating mechanism between the government, the ethnic groups and the international community for the implementation of the ceasefire agreements and the furthering of the peace processes.

Amongst the ethnic groups it is important to distinguish between their political and military wings with often divergent agendas and ideological positions. Those different views can also be traced back to the fact that most ethnic nationalities consist of sub-groups as well as splinter groups which makes the ethnic landscape rather complex.

The Burmese military is a further actor that needs special attention. As an institution, it proclaims itself to be supportive of reforms, but in reality, it remains rather unyielding when it comes to the many peace processes. For several years the military was not encouraged to function as a collegiate, but was composed of individual commanders responsible to a chief commander, with a strong top-down approach, in order to avoid any kind of alternative centres of power. Although it is no longer obvious how much control the chief commanders have in reality and how autonomous the individual commanders are, the military's involvement in the ceasefire discussions at the regional level remains decisive for the implementation of possible ceasefire agreements.

Although Aung San Suu Kyi is a key political actor, neither the ethnic groups nor the government see her as a central figure in the actual peace negotiations. Two roles could nevertheless be envisaged for her: to promote the peace agenda more generally as a national issue in Myanmar, and to voice these issues to the outside world.

In terms of the international community, Myanmar has hosted different international actors with divergent agendas over the years. On the one hand, there are those actors who simplistically can be viewed as 'Myanmar's old friends', particularly China, and on the other hand the new 'Western block' which includes donors, intergovernmental and non-governmental organizations. While Myanmar's old friends send mixed messages in regard to the peace processes, the Western block seems supportive of reforms and local organizations' initiatives. Generally, the international community has the potential to play an important bridging role between different local actors engaging in the peace processes of Myanmar, which still experiences low trust due to the ethnically fractured society.

The international community's involvement has been proved fruitful at the civil society level, where cooperation between several local and international NGOs has been playing an important role at different tracks in the peace processes. Notably, they facilitate contacts, bring expertise and build capacity of parties. The most significant civil society actors are: the *Nyein (Shalom) Foundation* (a national NGO), *Hope International*, the *Centre for Humanitarian Dialogue* (HD), the *Center for Peace and Conflict Studies* (CPCS) and the *Euro Burma Office* (EBO). They are all part of the *International Peace Support Group* (IPSG)—including the national ones—which aims to coordinate the efforts of both national and international actors engaged in the peace processes.[4] Additional coordination mechanisms in support of peace are: the *Peace Donor Support Group* (PDSG), composed of Norway, Australia, the UK, EU, World Bank and the UN; the *Working Group on Ethnic Coordination* (a coordination mechanism for ethnic armed groups)[5]; and the Norwegian-led *Myanmar Peace Support Initiative*.

International interventions have come into play at a stage in Myanmar's reform process, where most of the local organizations working on peace are still in the making. Myanmar's civil society has been building local capacity since 2008 on issues such as livelihood, health, education, and human rights. However to link these issues with the opening of the 'peace door' still remains a challenge for many local organizations. Thus, while one can find a vibrant civil society in Myanmar,

[4] The IPSG, founded in January 2012, is an informal grouping of international and national actors involved in assisting and advising the parties to ethnic conflict in Myanmar. It meets on a regular basis, both to review the situation and coordinate efforts to support durable peace processes. Members of the IPSG agree on the need for national stakeholders to own the peace process in Myanmar and have come together to aid and assist in a spirit of consultation, transparency and collaboration. They also deploy international experts to support and observe the negotiations between the ethnic groups and the government (taken from the draft TORs of the IPSG).

[5] EBO acts as their Secretariat.

few have extensive experience on peace issues. This lack is coupled with the absence of strong middle management leaders, which also complicates local capacity building. In such a context, the international community has the potential to fill the gap in both physical and technical support through the delivery of specific expertise on how to link issues such as business development, environmental conservation and security sector reform with broader peace issues. Furthermore, experiences of peacemaking from other countries may also be used as a tool to develop and strengthen local peace processes.

The strong presence of international actors in Myanmar can however become problematic if it compromises local ownership of peacebuilding and peacemaking and if processes lack inclusivity. Indeed an influx of different international 'peace businesses' into Myanmar may even distort the current peace processes. In this context, the Myanmar government has given clear signals that peacemaking should remain a domestic issue with no external facilitator. At the civil society level, concerns about the international community's involvement are voiced to a lesser extent. This silence may relate to the country's long struggle for international recognition and support. Military rule and international sanctions had made access to funding and resources from the international community extremely difficult. It is only in the past 2 years that Western countries have temporarily suspended sanctions and contributed towards a major push of donor aid in the country. The current lack of middle management, human resources and technical knowledge related to peace processes contributes to a wider acceptance of international actors amongst civil society groups. It should however be kept in mind that the strong presence of the international community and many newcomers may run the risk of constituting a relationship of dependency instead of complementarity.

Complementarity can only be guaranteed if international actors do not impose pre-conceived concepts on local actors but rather play a supportive role of already existing local efforts. A deep understanding of the complexity of Myanmar's conflict and peace processes as well as the dynamics between the actors may not only make the international community's support more likely to succeed but also prevent international actors from impeding current local peacemaking efforts. Additionally, it remains important to engage all these different potential peace actors in order to pursue an inclusive and locally owned peace. These different factors need to be taken into account before Myanmar becomes too 'crowded' with international organisations. For the time being, the provision of technical assistance and human resources may be a way for international actors to make a valuable contribution, however only if capacity-building, coordination and complementarity are respected. The following section describes one case of a successful cooperation between a Swiss and a Myanmar NGO, which serves as an example of best practice, as both local ownership and inclusivity have been pursued in a constructive and organic way.

7.3 Nyein (Shalom) Foundation and Swisspeace: Model of Cooperation Between a National and an International NGO

The partnership between the *Swiss Peace Foundation* (swisspeace) and the *Nyein (Shalom) Foundation* (NSF) based in Myanmar constitutes a specific model of cooperation between a national and an international NGO, which responds to local ownership and inclusiveness. The cooperation resulted from an in-depth conflict analysis of Myanmar conducted by the *Mediation Support Project* (MSP).[6] The MSP's analysis revealed that one of the best ways to engage in early peace efforts in Myanmar would be to support knowledge exchange and capacity building of local peacemaking activities. This was also linked to a growing demand from active local actors who were reaching out for specific support (for example on questions of how to strengthen public participation in peace processes) to allow them to play a meaningful role in the transformation of their country. As a consequence, swisspeace decided to second one of its mediation experts to the *NSF* from March to May 2012.

The *NSF*, with its coordinating office in Yangon, has been active in peace promotion since 2001, when the military regime was still in power. In the current context, it particularly focuses on the inclusiveness of peace processes, helping for instance to bring the voices of youth and women to the peace table. *NSF* has recently been involved in projects which attempt to bridge the different tracks of negotiation efforts. A major tool in this regard has been public consultations where accounts of grievances were collected at the grassroots level by local organizations. These actors subsequently made concrete recommendations for armed groups and the local authorities, which were then submitted back to *NSF*. This project was conducted in several regions in the country and has the potential to be replicated in further processes. In addition, *NSF* created the *Civil Society Forum for Peace* in 2012 to bridge, and facilitate dialogue between, civil society actors active in supporting peace at the different levels.

The mandate and purpose of the swisspeace secondment was to support the ongoing efforts of the *NSF* and, if needed and feasible, to also support that of additional actors involved in peace promotion in Myanmar. The overall objective was to strengthen local mediation capacity notably by providing expertise on peace negotiations and mediation; providing expertise on public participation in peace processes as well as on the role of the private sector in peace processes; contributing to training in negotiation techniques and mediation; and supporting the *NSF* and other local actors on the ground when needed in their ongoing activities to promote peace at the different stages of the conflict.

---

[6] MSP is a joint project between swisspeace and the ETH/CSS, funded by the Swiss Federal Department of Foreign Affairs.

More concretely, the contribution of swisspeace to the *NSF*'s activities was at two levels. Firstly, at the policy level, through collaborative engagement. This included working together on elaborating *NSF*'s strategy on how to effectively support the peace processes; reflecting on their current activities and recommending possible future ones; advising on how to coordinate and collaborate with international peace supporters and providing analysis and options on ways to conduct public participation in peace processes. Secondly, at the programme level through capacity building and knowledge transfer. This was done by conducting several trainings on public participation for *NSF* staff and supporting their integration into actual activities; organizing and facilitating seminars and workshops on 'Women and Peace' in Yangon and Chiang Mai; and facilitating a session on Business and Peace for members of the 'Peace Circle Network'. The current *NSF* projects on public participation and on the necessity to include women at the peace table are, for example, results of this collaboration.

Three concrete examples demonstrate how local ownership was ensured in this partnership. Firstly, most of the training was jointly designed, with swisspeace bringing theory and examples from other cases and *NSF* integrating the context specific elements for Myanmar. Most presentations were done by the *NSF*, mainly in Burmese, with a representative of swisspeace present as a resource person. Secondly, swisspeace'*s* several guidance notes on specific themes related to conducting peace negotiations (e.g. power sharing, dealing with the past, how to constructively include the private sector etc.) were shared with the *NSF*. In-depth discussions and brainstorming complemented those documents, with the *NSF* then having the space to use relevant documents and training to feed into their discussions with parties at the peace table. Finally, the idea to establish a Civil Society Forum emerged after the *NSF*'s Assistant Director, Ja Nan Lahtaw, attended a peace mediation course[7] in Switzerland in June 2012. The course was useful in highlighting the need to bridge the different tracks of the peace process. The support, exchange and discussions she had during and after that course helped the *NSF* to create and implement the *Civil Society Forum for Peace* in an approach that was relevant for the Myanmar current context.

The joint project between swisspeace and the *NSF* can be deemed a unique approach, where local mediation capacity and peace negotiations expertise have been strengthened through secondment. The idea to send an international staff member to a local NGO in the field of peace promotion was recognized by many actors as a creative model and the perfect fit given the context and dynamics on the ground. Indeed, leaving national actors in the 'driving seat' yet providing the space for internationals to support specific needs (for example bringing examples from other peace negotiation experiences) has proved to be effective. In addition, the secondment experience allowed the swisspeace expert to find a balance between

[7] The peace mediation course mentioned here takes place once a year in Switzerland and is funded by the Swiss Federal Department of Foreign Affairs. For more information please visit: http://peacemediation.ch.

being integrated into the *NSF*'s activities and the freedom to conduct independent research and assessments. The *MSP* intends to continue to work closely with local entities in order to support a nationally driven peace effort. Follow-up projects are already taking place and the collaboration will continue in the future.

7.4 Context for an International Engagement in Myanmar Today

This last section presents a few important elements to consider when planning for any future international engagement in the current Myanmar context.

1. Given their history and a certain 'national pride', Myanmar leaders from both government and ethnic groups generally want to be in the 'driver's seat' in terms of reforms and peace processes. They do not expect internationals to play a third party role or to dictate activities.

   Recommendation: Strong respect for local ownership. The role that the international community should continue to play is one of an assistant for local peace supporters, be it for the government negotiation team, the ethnic groups or the local entities facilitating the processes.

2. There is a serious lack of institutional and technical capacity in the country. Much decision-making is rushed and ad hoc as human and time resources are scarce. The demand for the time of senior policymakers in all spheres of society is high and this has intensified with many international agencies coming to Myanmar and accessing key resource persons. The lack of capacity at the mid-level and working level to implement policy decisions is also a major challenge.

   Recommendation: Secondments of experts should be further explored in the short term in order to build capacity and support national actors at all levels of society. The international community should not put all its eggs in one basket and should rather diversify its support both in their selection of organizations and in their forms of support.

3. During the last 18 months numerous international actors have arrived in the country, making it difficult for local actors to remain up to date on all of their different intentions, roles and activities.

   Recommendation: Coordination and collaboration should lead any activities in the country in order to avoid mixed messages and the duplication of efforts. Using the current coordination mechanisms seems helpful.

4. Myanmar has a vibrant civil society that has existed for many years and has been operating in a very restricted environment.

   Recommendation: Reinforce and empower existing local NGOs and other civil society actors instead of 'starting from scratch' with new actors. Mapping actors and a capacity assessment could be a useful first step.

5. Those engaged in the peace processes need support from both inside and outside to continue to maintain their space to push the peace agenda forward.

Recommendation: Identify and support 'agents of change' notably in civil society, ethnic groups and the diaspora as well as 'reformers' in the current government as key change makers. Close consultations with and support of the reformers in the government is essential. At the same time, one must reflect on how too much exposure of reformers has the potential to put them at risk of internal competition. Furthermore, reflections on how to engage the state army in the peace processes are also crucial.

6. The pace of reforms and peace processes has been amazingly rapid. Too rapid for some while raising concerns for others.

Recommendation: Internationals need to be present while accompanying the national rhythm of the opening. However, the rapidity of the transition also requires regularly drawing lessons from recent experiences and allowing some reflection prior to acting, while also assisting national counterparts to stand back and to take stock as well. A healthy 'step back and breathe' is likely to help prevent mistakes.

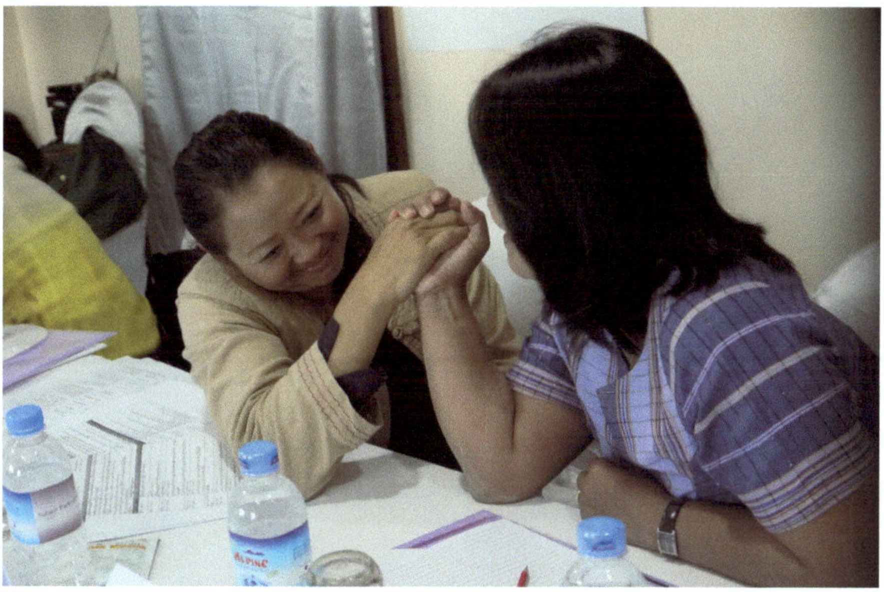

Participants at a negotiation training in Yangon, Myanmar. *Source* Rachel Gasser/ swisspeace. Permission was granted to publish this photo.

Those engaged in the peace processes need support from both inside and outside to continue to maintain their space to push the peace [illegible]

Concluding Remarks

This book has offered insights into the balance between external interventions and locally led initiatives. The theoretically-based contributions bear testimony to the relevance that the concept of local ownership has gained in peacebuilding and development debates. At the same time, they point to the conceptual limitations of the term as well as the practical challenges of meaningfully implementing it.

Conceptually, the authors show how local ownership has become a buzzword for donors and a largely externally-driven concept: sometimes it has become simply a means to promote local compliance with international norms and mainly relevant from an international perspective focusing on the 'buy-in' of local actors to pre-conceived projects. Practically, they agree that many peacebuilding programmes continue to be designed and implemented without substantial local inputs. They demonstrate how a thorough implementation of local ownership has often stumbled over difficulties of identification of local counterparts in highly heterogeneous constituencies, convincing tax payers to invest in locally led projects, or overcoming UN member states' resistance to handing over responsibility for peace processes.

In light of these challenges, all the authors suggest refinements of the concept. Hellmüller suggests a middle ground between liberal and communitarian approaches highlighting the need for a context-specific assessment of the interaction between external and internal peacebuilding actors based on their respective comparative advantages. Schuman proposes political ownership as key to integrating local perspectives in the analysis of the conflict and to guarantee an internally negotiated solution to end civil war. Pfister argues that a focus on inclusiveness coupled with a more 'honest dialogue' would lead to a more respectful interaction between local and international actors. While all the authors propose amendments to the concept of local ownership, the baby should not be thrown out with the bathwater. Rather, all three authors' contributions suggest that instead of hiding behind the buzzword of local ownership, a more in-depth inquiry into how local and international actors can best work together for peace is needed.

Analyses of this interaction are provided by the case studies. They highlight the significance of the local level as well as its complexity. They suggest identifying local counterparts based on the local population's perceptions of legitimate actors,

S. Hellmüller and M. Santschi (eds.), *Is Local Beautiful?*,
SpringerBriefs in Environment, Security, Development and Peace 11,
DOI: 10.1007/978-3-319-00306-1, © The Author(s) 2014

institutions and organizations, rather than looking for like-minded persons or succumbing to international assessments of legitimacy or administrative standards.

The case studies point to the manifold actors working for peace at the local level. Be it the wide ranging local conflict resolution efforts by chiefs and other traditional authorities in South Sudan, the Centre Résolution Conflits' DDR projects in North Kivu and Ituri or the peace promotion activities by the Nyein (Shalom) Foundation in Myanmar: they all testify to the vast amount of local capacities for peace present in those contexts. International actors should support these initiatives already undertaken locally, rather than substitute or duplicate them. Their role can be in capacity-building in specific areas of expertise (thematic and administrative), in providing logistical support or in increasing the leverage of local organizations who often work at small scales. Thereby, the authors of the case studies unanimously underline the importance of complementarity of local and international actors.

At the same time, norms and values need to be negotiated. With her case study of South Sudan, Santschi illustrates the spheres of social interaction between local, national and international actors with sometimes divergent perceptions on specific institutions and practices. The two discussed examples of 'grassroots' peace conferences illustrate that 'local' peace processes are often intertwined with national political processes and supported by international actors. Ambassador Wild also provides insights into these negotiation processes in cases where western norms do not correspond to local ones. While concessions should never be made on values or principles, such as human rights or the rule of law, he suggests that we should be flexible with regard to administrative standards.

Gasser/Lahtaw and Hayman provide specific recommendations for the way forward. Hayman focuses on how donors, INGOs and local NGOs can maximize the potential of locally led peacebuilding. Gasser/Lahtaw present examples of how international actors can best support the current peace process in Myanmar. All the case studies give us highly valuable insights into best practices and lessons learnt from a wide range of perspectives and cases. At the same time, they indicate that the implementation of local ownership remains highly context-specific. Thus, the most important finding of the book is that the equilibrium between external interventions and locally led peacebuilding needs to be found in every setting anew.

Sara Hellmüller
Heinz Krummenacher
Martina Santschi

On swisspeace

swisspeace is an action-oriented peace research institute with headquarters in Bern, Switzerland. It aims to prevent the outbreak of violent conflicts and to enable sustainable conflict transformation.

swisspeace sees itself as a center of excellence and an information platform in the areas of conflict analysis and peacebuilding. We conduct research on the causes of war and violent conflict, develop tools for early recognition of tensions, and formulate conflict mitigation and peacebuilding strategies. swisspeace contributes to information exchange and networking on current issues of peace and security policy through its analyses and reports as well as meetings and conferences.

swisspeace was founded in 1988 as the "Swiss Peace Foundation" with the goal of promoting independent peace research in Switzerland. Today swisspeace engages about 40 staff members. Its most important clients include the Swiss Federal Department of Foreign Affairs (FDFA) and the Swiss National Science Foundation. Its activities are further assisted by contributions from its Support Association. The supreme swisspeace body is the Foundation Council, which is comprised of representatives from politics, science, and the government.

swisspeace is an associated Institute of the University of Basel and member of the Swiss Academy of Humanities and Social Sciences (SAHS).

Links:

- www.swisspeace.ch
- http://www.swisspeace.ch/activities/events/annual-conferences.html
- https://www.facebook.com/pages/swisspeace/421002731270405
- http://archivesproject.swisspeace.ch/
- http://businessconflictcheck.swisspeace.ch/en/
- http://koff.swisspeace.ch/
- http://peacemediation.ch/

S. Hellmüller and M. Santschi (eds.), *Is Local Beautiful?*,
SpringerBriefs in Environment, Security, Development and Peace 11,
DOI: 10.1007/978-3-319-00306-1, © The Author(s) 2014

Authors' Biographies

Rachel Gasser

Rachel Gasser is a Mediation Programme Officer at swisspeace. Her main responsibilities are advising parties to a conflict, supporting third party mediation and conducting applied research on issues related to peace mediation. She has been involved in West Africa, Central Asia and South East Asia. She currently supports the activities of a local Myanmar NGO in the peace processes. Previous work experiences include the UN Department of Political Affairs in New York, the Centre for Applied Studies in International Negotiations (CASIN), the Swiss Mission to the UN and UNHCR. She studied at the Graduate Institute of International Studies in Geneva and at UC Berkeley, USA. She holds a Master from the Graduate Institute.

Address: Sonnenbergstrasse 17, P.O. Box, CH-3000 Bern 7
Website: http://www.swisspeace.ch/aboutus/staff-by-alphabetical-order/rachel-gasser.html
Email: rachel.gasser@swisspeace.ch

Carolyn Hayman

Carolyn Hayman founded together with Scilla Elworthy Peace Direct in 2004. Peace Direct funds and promotes local peacebuilding in conflict areas, providing resources and profile to outstanding local peace initiatives. Carolyn Hayman previously worked for the Foyer Federation, a network of projects providing accommodation and education for homeless young people. During this time she was also a Board member of the Commonwealth Development Corporation. She

S. Hellmüller and M. Santschi (eds.), *Is Local Beautiful?*,
SpringerBriefs in Environment, Security, Development and Peace 11,
DOI: 10.1007/978-3-319-00306-1, © The Author(s) 2014

acted as Joint Managing Director of the Korda Seed Capital Fund. She also worked in the consultancy business on office automation, for the Ministry of Overseas Development and as a member of the UK Cabinet Office Think Tank. She graduated from Cambridge University and holds a Master in Development Economics.

Address: Peace Direct, 56 Leonard Street, London EC2A 4LT
Website: http://www.peacedirect.org/about/who-we-are/
Email: carolyn@peacedirect.org

Sara Hellmüller

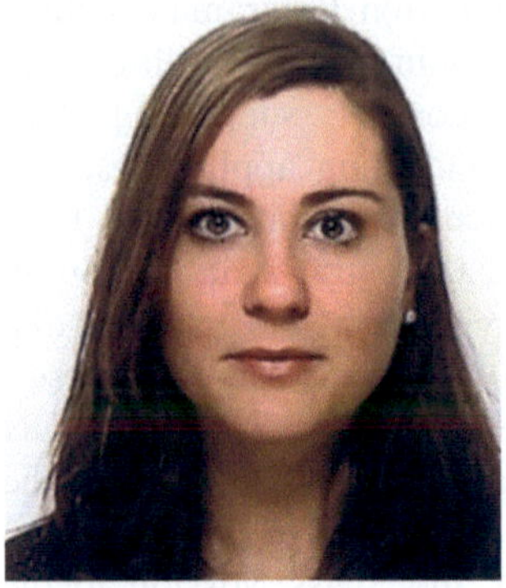

Sara Hellmüller is a PhD Candidate at the University of Basel and a Programme Officer in the Mediation Programme at swisspeace. She holds a Master Degree in International Relations from the Graduate Institute of International Studies in Geneva and a Master of Law and Diplomacy from the Fletcher School at Tufts University in Boston. Previous work experiences include internships with UNDP in eastern Congo, with the Swiss Embassy in Abuja, with local NGOs in Mongolia and South Africa. She is currently writing her PhD dissertation on the interaction between local and international actors in peacebuilding in the Democratic Republic of Congo.

Address: Sonnenbergstrasse 17, P.O. Box, CH-3000 Bern 7
Website: http://www.swisspeace.ch/aboutus/staff/staff-by-alphabetical-order/sara-hellmueller.html
Email: sara.hellmueller@swisspeace.ch

Heinz Krummenacher

Heinz Krummenacher received his MA (1982) and PhD (1985) in political science from the University of Zurich. He started his professional career with the Swiss Defence Department where he directed a study group dealing with the re-definition of Swiss security policy (1985–1989). Between 1990 and 1992 he served as foreign editor with the Swiss daily newspaper *Der Bund*. Before joining swisspeace in 1998 he was head of the social research and media department at IHA-GfK, a leading market research institute (1992–1998). At swisspeace he was head of the early warning programme FAST International (1998–2008) and is, since 2001, a member of the directorate. In addition, he is the CEO of the BEFORE project.

Address: Sonnenbergstrasse 17, P.O. Box, CH-3000 Bern 7
Website: http://www.swisspeace.ch/aboutus/staff/staff-by-alphabetical-order/heinz-krummenacher.html
Email: heinz.krummenacher@swisspeace.ch

Jan Nan Lahtaw

Ja Nan Lahtaw is Assistant Director for Programmes and International Relations of Shalom (Nyein) Foundation in Myanmar. Her main responsibilities are designing the peace programmes of the organization, networking with international communities, local organizations and facilitating peacebuilding trainings with various religious and social organizations and ethnic groups. Ja Nan holds a M.A in conflict transformation from Eastern Mennonite University (VA), USA. She was a Chevening Fellow (2008) at Birmingham University, UK. She has taught at the Master of Applied Conflict Transformation Studies programme (ACTS) of Pannasastra University in conjunction with the Center for Peace and Conflict Studies in Cambodia. She is also an active member of Action Asia, a Network of Peace Builders in Asia region.

Address: No. 95 A, Penthouse, Shaw Padauk Condo, Myay Nu Street, San Chaung, Yangon, Myanmar
Website: http://www.shalommyanmar.org/
Email: Janan.shalom@gmail.com

Marco Pfister

Marco Pfister holds a Licence in International Relations from the Graduate Institute of International Studies in Geneva and an MA in Conflict Resolution and Post-Conflict Assistance from the Fletcher School of Law and Diplomacy in Boston, USA. He works at swisspeace in the Statehood and Conflict Programme focusing on questions of democratization and citizen participation in post-conflict statebuilding. Previous work experiences in Sudan include the management of a civil society-support programme and of an in-kind programme for local government and civil society in support of the peace process. He also served as strategic advisor to the Three Areas Steering Group in Sudan, a group of ten donor countries implementing programmes in Abyei, Southern Kordofan and Blue Nile.

Address: Waldheimstrasse 28, 3012 Bern
Email: marco.pfister@gmail.com

Martina Santschi

Martina Santschi holds an MA in Social Anthropology, Ecology and Biology from the University of Bern. She joined swisspeace in April 2007 as a PhD candidate and conducts research through NCCR North-South. The topic of her PhD research is "Negotiating Authority and Statehood in South Sudan". She has been involved in research projects and consultancies including for the Swiss Federal Department of Foreign Affairs and the Rift Valley Institute together with the United States Institute for Peace. Since 2012 she is also researcher with the Secure Livelihoods Research Consortium research project on South Sudan.

Address: Sonnenbergstrasse 17, P.O. Box, CH-3000 Bern 7
Website: http://www.swisspeace.ch/aboutus/staff/martina-santschi.html
Email: martina.santschi@swisspeace.ch

Peter Schumann

Peter Schuman studied at the University Mannheim in Germany. He started his overseas career in 1973 with German bilateral aid programmes. He joined the UN in 1979, worked with ILO and UNFPA and became a UNDP staff member in 1983. With UNDP he specialized in programmes in support of war and civil strife affected countries and worked in India, Pakistan, Sri Lanka, Sudan, Mozambique, Liberia, Somalia, Tajikistan and Albania. He was seconded to UN peace operations in Iraq, Kosovo and Sudan. At the end of 2007 he joined the University Konstanz. He conducts field trips to Sudan and South Sudan, provides training for personnel seconded to the UN and other peace operations and advises on policy issues.

Address: Clara-Wieck-Str. 5, 10785 Berlin
Email: schumannp@t-online.de

Ambassador Claude Wild

Ambassador Claude Wild completed his studies in political science and international relations and post-graduate studies in security policy at the Graduate Institute of International and Development Studies in Geneva. Before joining the Swiss diplomatic service, he participated in UN peace operations in Namibia and Western Sahara. As a diplomat, he has worked e.g. with the Swiss Agency for Development and Cooperation and the Swiss embassy in Nigeria. He was deputy head of the peace-policy section of UN and International Organizations Division in Berne, first secretary and counsellor at the Swiss embassy in Moscow, and in charge of the policy and institutions section of the Directorate for European Affairs in Bern. In August 2010, he was appointed Ambassador and head of the FDFA's Human Security Division.

Address: Federal Department of Foreign Affairs, Directorate of Political Affairs, Human Security Division, Bundesgasse 32, 3003 Bern

About the Book

Based on the swisspeace annual conference 2012, this book examines the delicate balance between international interventions and locally led initiatives. It examines how local ownership—emerging as key criteria for any external intervention—is constituted: does this concept only imply local participation or is local control from the outset a must? Moreover, it addresses the question of what 'local' means in the peacebuilding and development context; which actors on the ground actually represent the local level and how external actors choose their partners from amongst them. Finally, it assesses the potential of locally led initiatives and local conflict resolution mechanisms and their interaction with external interventions. Several authors provide insights on these issues and nuance our thinking about both local ownership and external interventions. As such, the publication aims to encourage critical reflections on this topical debate in peacebuilding and development.

S. Hellmüller and M. Santschi (eds.), *Is Local Beautiful?*,
SpringerBriefs in Environment, Security, Development and Peace 11,
DOI: 10.1007/978-3-319-00306-1, © The Author(s) 2014

MIX
Papier aus verantwortungsvollen Quellen
Paper from responsible sources
FSC® C105338

If you have any concerns about our products,
you can contact us on
ProductSafety@springernature.com

In case Publisher is established outside the EU,
the EU authorized representative is:
Springer Nature Customer Service Center GmbH
Europaplatz 3, 69115 Heidelberg, Germany

Printed by Libri Plureos GmbH
in Hamburg, Germany